Interviewing the Sexually Abused Child

Investigation of Suspected Abuse

DAVID P. H. JONES

Interviewing the Sexually Abused Child

Investigation of Suspected Abuse

GASKELL

Gaskell is an imprint of the Royal College of Psychiatrists,
17 Belgrave Square, London SW1

British Library Cataloguing-in-Publication Data
Jones, David P. H.
    Interviewing the Sexually Abused Child:
    Investigation of Suspected Abuse.—
    4Rev.ed
    I. Title
    362.7

ISBN 0-902241-46-X 4th edition
(ISBN 0-902241-23-0 3rd edition)

Distributed in North America
by American Psychiatric Press, Inc.
ISBN 0-880486-12-0

First published 1985 by the University of Colorado
    School of Medicine
Second edition 1986
Third edition published 1988 by Gaskell
Reprinted with amendments 1989
Fourth edition 1992

Typeset by Dobbie Typesetting Limited, Tavistock, Devon
Printed in Great Britain

Contents

Acknowledgements   vi

Introduction   vii

1 The predicament of the child sexual-abuse victim   1

2 The contribution of psychological research   11

3 Preliminary considerations   19

4 Screening for the possibility of sexual abuse   26

5 The interview itself   30

6 The process of validation   51

Appendices A Suggested contents for an interviewing room   57

B Resources for the interviewer   59

References   62

Acknowledgements

It is impossible to acknowledge individually all the many people, including professional colleagues and abused and non-abused children, who have provided help and understanding in the writing of this book. I am particularly indebted to friends and colleagues in Denver who were so encouraging during the book's inception stages between 1982 and 1984. In particular I wish to mention Dr Richard Krugman from the C. Henry Kempe National Center for the Prevention and Treatment of Child Abuse, and Dr Gail Goodman who was then at the University of Denver, as well as Mrs Mary McQuiston who helped me prepare the first edition. Numerous helpful comments have been received since the first edition which have been useful in revisions of new editions. An anonymous review obtained in preparation for the third edition was valuable and helped to shape the subsequent approach. Above all, I am grateful to all those who have commented on it and with whom I have discussed the complexities of interviewing children who are suspected victims of sexual abuse.

DAVID JONES

Introduction

Although instances of what may now be described as child sexual abuse (CSA) were described in the book of Genesis, the burgeoning of professional interest has been a relatively recent phenomenon. Freud's case histories of his 'adult survivors' remain vivid descriptions, even today, but he superseded them with more acceptable theories of infantile sexuality and fantasy. There was a marked increase in interest about the physical abuse and neglect of children in the 1960s, and this was followed by a similar concern with sexual abuse in the 1970s and 1980s. The basis for the conclusion that a child has been physically abused remains the identification of inadequately explained injuries, while that of neglect rests upon the observation of deprived standards of parental care with consequent ill effects upon the child's development. Sexual abuse is significantly different from these two. Recognition of sexual abuse depends upon hearing what the child has to say, and less frequently on physical examination or findings. The child's account is of prime importance, which is why this publication has been prepared. The interview with the child is of crucial relevance to clinicians, police, and courts. This short book has been produced as a handbook to help those who talk with children who may have been sexually abused.

The assessment of possible cases involving CSA has come under scrutiny in all countries where the problem of CSA is being increasingly recognised and addressed. The UK is no exception, and, at the time of preparing the third edition, the country was assimilating the conclusions of the Cleveland Child Abuse Inquiry (Butler-Sloss, 1988). The report emphasised that an assessment of possible cases of CSA must follow principles of accepted good practice already existing in the fields of child psychology, psychiatry, and child-welfare work. The interview with the child had to be supplemented by inquiries into other areas of the child's life, including family life. In order to achieve an adequate assessment, high-quality multidisciplinary working practices were of primary importance (Butler-Sloss, 1988). The recommendations and practices described in this book are intended to complement, rather than substitute, the procedures and practices of the individual professional disciplines. Furthermore, the way in which the interview with the child fits in with other parts of the multidisciplinary process of assessment must be worked out on a local basis, aided by the establishment and publication of agreed, written procedures to be followed in response to suspicions of child abuse (Bross *et al*, 1988; Department of Health, 1991). The author's hope is that this publication will be of value to medical practitioners, social workers, police, nurses, and others who have to talk in detail with children. A working knowledge of child-development issues is assumed as this is necessary for working professionally with children.

Why write a special publication on interviewing the sexually abused child? After all, surely sexually abused children are just the same as any other troubled children? My answer is that, even though the principles involved in interviewing children about their psychological problems may be familiar ones, there are issues specific to the child who has been sexually abused, which warrant a special publication. These issues include the psychology of child victims of abuse and maltreatment, the context of maltreatment, children's memory, and the link between professional clinical practice and the legal system. Therefore, in order to consider interviewing children who may have been abused, wider knowledge and experience are required than are needed for talking with other troubled children. The book is organised in the following way.

Chapter 1 describes the pressures that come to bear upon the child victim, both within the family and from the system outside. These pressures can be considered by examining how the problem presents to professionals. For example, the presentation may follow a single abusive incident or may occur after many years of intrafamilial incest. The resulting pressure on the child differs greatly between these extremes, especially as the child may be perhaps 3 or 13 years old when the abuse is disclosed. A working knowledge of these pressures helps the interviewer to appreciate how different the children are who are unified by the experience of being sexually victimised. There is a growing appreciation of the dynamics of victimisation, which has been derived from the study of victims of child abuse, spouse abuse, and other violent crimes. A knowledge of this area is a prerequisite to approaching child sexual-abuse victims, and is outlined on pages 7–9.

Interviews are conducted within the context of the available research in the field. Recent developments in the fields of cognitive psychology, the memory ability of young children, the child as witness, children's 'suggestibility', language, and knowledge of sexuality should be incorporated into practice. Relevant aspects of these areas of inquiry are reviewed in Chapter 2.

Chapters 3, 4, and 5 cover the interview itself. In Chapter 3, important preliminary considerations are considered, including the setting for the interview, the presence of parents, and when and how the session can be recorded. The author assumes that in each area there are policies about who should interview the child suspected of having been sexually abused. Even if these are clear and agreed by the local professional community, not all suspicion will warrant a full-scale interview. In many cases sexual abuse is one of a series of possible considerations, hence Chapter 4 is concerned with screening for the possibility of CSA. Hopefully this will be helpful to general clinicians in a range of professional settings.

Chapter 5 deals with the investigative interview. The approach can be equated with that recommended in the UK in the *Memorandum of Good Practice: Video Recorded Interviews with Child Witnesses for Criminal Proceedings* (Home Office, 1992) which forms part of the Criminal Justice Act 1991. The Memorandum is in draft form at the time of going to press. Although the Memorandum is primarily concerned with the interviewing of children in criminal cases, it is also expected to influence the conduct of interviews in civil cases. For these reasons the present edition has been revised to ensure that the reader can apply the suggestions made in this book within the framework of the Memorandum.

Finally, validation is a crucial issue both for clinicians and the courts – is the child giving a truthful account? In Chapter 6, a clinical approach to validation is presented.

This book does not attempt to cover all the areas relevant to interviewing sexually abused children. The reader is referred to more general texts that cover interviewing and diagnostic assessment of children to place this book's focus on sexual abuse into context (Cox & Rutter, 1985; Hill, 1985). The assessment of mental status or the psychological impact of abuse is not covered. I do not cover the entire field of abuse and neglect of children, and again refer the reader to more general texts for this (e.g. Mrazek & Kempe, 1981; Sgroi, 1982; Helfer & Kempe, 1987). This book's focus is on the investigative interview. This fourth edition has involved a full revision of the entire text. It is a reflection of the speed of developments in the field that this has been necessary. Although the overall direction and approach remains the same, much of the detail has been revised. The primary orientation of the book remains, to guide those who need to know if a child has or has not been sexually abused.

1 The predicament of the child sexual-abuse victim

This chapter is concerned with the pressures and influences that affect the victims. This clinical understanding can help us to appreciate the predicament the victims find themselves in (Taylor, 1982), enabling us to understand better the child whom we are interviewing.

Before the predicament of the victim is described further, we must define child sexual abuse (CSA). The most frequently quoted definition is that provided by Schechter & Roberge (1976): "the involvement of dependent, developmentally immature children and adolescents in sexual activities that they do not fully comprehend, and are unable to give informed consent to and that violate the social taboos of family roles". A shorter working definition has been provided by Fraser (1981): "the exploitation of a child for the sexual gratification of an adult". These definitions are useful pointers to the general area of concern, but they lack specificity and practical applicability. Locally, we have therefore preferred to use a definition that is operational and that specifically describes the terms of reference (Oxfordshire Area Child Protection Committee, 1992). It is based on the approaches of Russell (1986), Finkelhor (1979), and Mrazek (1981).

"Child Sexual Abuse

Actual or likely occurrence of a sexual act(s)[1] perpetrated on a child by another person. Children cannot give consent because of their dependent condition. However the question of consent may be more complex with older children, or when there is a small age gap between 'abuser' and 'abused'. The key issue in assessing whether sexual abuse has occurred is that of exploitation[2].

[1]*Sexual Act(s)*

(i) Direct
– genital or anal sexual contact between child and adult.
– penetration – anal, vaginal or oral.
– other acts where the child is the object of the adult's sexual gratification
  (e.g. bondage, frotteurism, ejaculation on to the child).

1

(ii) Indirect
- genital exposure.
- production of pornographic material.
- encouraging two children to have sex together.
- exposing children to pornographic materials.

2Exploitation

The balance of power between the child and the other person at the time when the sexual activity first occurred. Thus exploitation is considered to have occurred if the activity was unwanted when it first began, and/or involved a misuse of conventional age, authority, or gender differentials.

As a secondary consideration the age difference between the two can be considered. When the suspected perpetrator is five or more years older than the child there will generally have been an exploitation of the age differential.''

In Oxfordshire we have decided to exclude the following activities from our definition of sexual abuse: verbal proposition or suggestion, and certain underage sex. In some situations a child under the age of 16 has had sexual intercourse with a person over 16 and from a legal perspective in the UK, unlawful sexual intercourse is said to have occurred. Using the above definition of sexual abuse, we are able to decide from a child-protection standpoint whether the activity should be considered as an example of sexual abuse. The key considerations will be the question of consent and the issue of exploitation.

Presentation

Children may disclose the fact that they have been sexually abused at many different points in their life. It is known from community surveys that many adults have never disclosed the fact that they have been sexually abused (Finkelhor, 1979; Russell, 1986). Historically, it is probable that the majority of victims did not tell anyone about their experience. However, we can describe some of the common presentations of the children who do tell.

People who have been sexually abused frequently delay reporting what has happened to them. Studies and case series consistently emphasise that delay is a major clinical feature of CSA cases (for example, see Meiselman, 1978; Finkelhor, 1979; Russell, 1986; Conte *et al*, 1987). There is less delay in reporting CSA committed by a stranger. Thus, CSA is brought to the attention of someone else besides the child and her[1] abuser. This process of 'disclosure' occurs at a variable period of time after the abuse has begun. Furthermore, for some children, CSA starts in infancy, while, for other

[1]The use of feminine and masculine pronouns is interchangeable throughout this book.

victims, abuse starts in teenage years. These variables notwithstanding, we can look at presentation both from the perspective of when the child presents and how presentation occurs.

Ounsted & Lynch (1976) first described the *Open warning* in the field of physical abuse, whereby the parents let a professional know, often in an ambiguous way, that all is not well within the home and that their child is in danger. They noted that the professional often responded by *Gaze aversion*, turning a blind eye to these and other warning signs. In sexual abuse, the situation is similar, but this time it is the child who tries to alert the world to his plight. The child may make an ambiguous statement, perhaps about "another little boy I know", ascribing his own experience to this other mythical child. Similarly, younger victims may simulate cunnilingus, fellatio, or even attempt intercourse with a friend while playing; this, too, may provide an open warning to a parent or professional. Older, more verbal children, may attempt to drop small hints about their experience to a trusted friend, schoolteacher or counsellor, or to a neighbour. Adolescents may run away for no apparent reason, perhaps hoping that someone will ask them the question that they have felt burdened with for a long time. All these expressions of distress may be understood as 'early' or 'open' warnings that sexual abuse may be occurring to the child in question.

Children may make far more direct statements to parents, relatives, adult or child friends, or to counsellors and teachers about sexual abuse. Unfortunately, that person may or may not listen to them. Many victims report being disbelieved or even admonished for their untruthfulness when they made their first disclosure of sexual abuse (Burgess & Holmstrom, 1975). The effect of such disbelief or inaction by a professional person may cause the victim to retain secrecy for many years. When a direct statement is made, it often occurs when the child feels comfortable; for example, during preparation for bedtime, or at bathtime. It seems that, at these times, the world feels relatively safe to the child, and perhaps also, the act of undressing facilitates talk about her own body. For example, one young child, when being bathed by a trusted parent, pointed to her genital area and said "daddy kisses my pee pee". Usually children disclose a small portion of their total experience initially, apparently in an attempt to test the adult's response before letting them know more about the assault. If they receive a positive and supportive response, they may feel safe enough to disclose more about their experience.

A change in behaviour is common when a child has been sexually abused. In general, children tend to respond to specific stresses in a non-specific way behaviourally. This is the case in child sexual abuse, too. The most common behavioural consequences in the victims are neurotic disorders or disturbances of conduct that may be of a relatively non-specific nature. There are, in addition, some more specific types of behaviour that occur in sexually abused children and may act as pointers to the possibility that sexual abuse is occurring (for a review, see Browne & Finkelhor, 1986). Some of these behavioural sequelae are discussed below under "The effects of child sexual abuse".

The first presentation of sexual abuse may be a physical illness. Venereal disease in prepubescent children strongly suggests sexual abuse (Neinstein *et al*, 1984). Some children present in hospital emergency rooms with physical evidence of an assault or rape (Royal College of Physicians, 1991). Frequent urinary-tract infections in girls without clear physical cause may also raise the question of child sexual abuse. Enuresis and encopresis are common accompaniments to child sexual abuse; however, studies to discover what proportion of young children with these latter problems are sexual-abuse victims have not been done yet. Inspection of the external genitalia of children suspected of abuse may be of value in the assessment (see Chapter 6). The Royal College of Physicians in the UK (Royal College of Physicians, 1991) and the American Academy of Pediatrics (1991) have issued consensus documents summarising the state of knowledge on the physical examination of children suspected of having been sexually abused.

Some young people present for the first time when they become pregnant (Mehta *et al*, 1979). Sometimes the adolescent becomes pregnant by her first boyfriend as a means to leave home or as a result of her promiscuity (Lukianowicz, 1972). On occasion, however the pregnancy is a result of incest. Such young people guard their secrets and do not disclose that the fathers of the children are, in fact, their own fathers or brothers. At this late stage in the biography of incest victims, they have become 'participants', and pregnancies resulting from incest are tangible and constant reminders of their feelings of guilt and shame.

For other children, the first presentation occurs when they cross to the other side of the fence and perpetrate the act to others. Their access to younger children may occur with peers in playgroup or school, or may occur for the first time when, as teenagers, they babysit young children (Meiselman, 1978; Becker & Abel, 1984).

Many victims do not present until adult life, and as such appear to be over-represented among the patients admitted to psychiatric hospitals (Gelinas, 1983), and among those attending sexual-dysfunction clinics. Additionally, incest victims are over-represented among those who injure themselves (Simpson & Porter, 1981), attempt suicide, turn to drugs and alcohol, and who become prostitutes (James & Meyerding, 1977).

Summarising, a person may present at various points throughout their life. Delay before disclosing sexual abuse is commonplace and may be extended for many years after the event. The presentations are frequently vague initially. There are five main ways in which children who have been sexually abused are discovered:

(a) through a spontaneous account by the child
(b) through disturbed behaviour or changes in behaviour exhibited by the child
(c) through the child's physical signs and symptoms

(d) through discovery of CSA when another form of maltreatment is being investigated
(e) through the suspicions of parents, relatives, or other adults about the child.

The most common mode of presentation is through the direct statement of the child (Conte *et al*, 1987). The first person whom a child normally tells is another child of similar age. The second commonest mode of presentation is for the child to tell a parent or trusted adult.

The effects of child sexual abuse

The predicament of the child sexual-abuse victim can also be understood by considering the behavioural effects of child victimisation in more detail. It has already been noted that children respond psychologically in a non-specific way to specific stressors. Further, CSA is not a unitary phenomenon but covers a wide variety of activities and situations. Thus, children who have been assaulted by a stranger on one occasion are grouped together with children who have been the victims of incest for many years before finally disclosing their plight, and all these are described as 'child sexual-abuse victims'. In addition to the heterogeneity of the experience itself to a child, there are additional factors to be considered. For example, any accompanying neglect, emotional abuse, deprivation, or even frank physical abuse, is likely to have a considerable effect on the final psychological state of the child. We also know that the extent of the child victim's involvement in pornography and 'sex ring' activity with others appears to have an influence upon outcome (Burgess *et al*, 1984). In fact a purely linear model of abuse and subsequent behaviour and emotional consequences is woefully inadequate. It ignores the importance of the child's pre-existing adjustment, the family context and their response to discovery of abuse, as well as any co-existing emotional abuse or neglect. All these factors contribute to the eventual psychological outcome for the child (see Friedrich, 1990, Chapters 1 and 2, for a useful discussion of the breadth of the impact of sexual abuse in context).

Most professionals who meet with child sexual-abuse victims observe the psychological sequelae of the sexual abuse in the weeks and months that follow disclosure of chronic abuse. By contrast, the psychological after-effects of the assault itself are usually only seen in those children who are the victims of a single assault by a stranger, and whose parents take them to a professional for help. The effects observed at these two points appear to be quite different. For example, the psychological after-effects of an acute assault are similar to those observed in adults following rape (Burgess & Holmstrom, 1974; Everstine & Everstine, 1983). The child shows symptoms of acute anxiety and agitation, with nightmares, night terrors, specific fears or phobias, and a fear of an attack. Guilt feelings are common, with depressed affect and sometimes a predominant feeling of helplessness. Gender and other sexual-identity problems may develop in boys who fear that they will now be homosexuals, and girls who become convinced that they are 'damaged goods' (Porter *et al*, 1982).

The effects seen after abuse has occurred repeatedly are variable (Gomes-Schwartz *et al*, 1985; Friedrich *et al*, 1987). As already stated, the most common reactions are non-specific, neurotic disorders or a deterioration in the child's conduct. Thus, children may become more anxious and fearful, be unable to concentrate and attend to their school work as well as they had, and show evidence of sleep and appetite disturbance. Similarly, other children show signs of withdrawal, and may be mildly depressed with guilty thoughts and the expression of more anger than is usual for their character. Some children's conduct deteriorates and they may begin to lie about everyday events, steal, or become aggressive with their friends. Preschool children may develop temper tantrums, whereas adolescents may 'act out' in a more dramatic and obvious fashion. They may become involved in drugs, make suicide attempts, run away, or simply become beyond the control of their parents or teachers. There is an association between teenage pregnancy, anorexia nervosa, teenage prostitution, and a history of sexual abuse. Sexual acting out behaviour occurs in a significant minority of sexually abused children. While such behaviour can be the consequence of other experiences, sexual abuse must be high on any diagnostician's list. The effect of CSA on the child's developing sexuality is especially grave. (For a full discussion see Jones & Thompson, 1991, and Friedrich, 1990.)

What proportion of children who are sexually abused and then disclose their abuse, show behavioural change in the subsequent weeks or months? Estimates and studies suggest that approximately two-thirds will show moderate or severe evidence of emotional or behavioural change of the types listed above (see, for example, Conte & Berliner, 1988). In the other one-third of children, there is either no, or else mild, psychological disturbance; however, we do not yet have the long-term follow-up studies to enable us to know how children in this latter group fare when they grow older. It is possible that this one-third of children will show delayed responses to CSA, or alternatively escape with few ill effects in the long term.

A significant number of children develop a post-traumatic stress disorder (American Psychiatric Association, 1980) after they have been sexually exploited (Conte & Berliner, 1988; McLeer *et al*, 1988). This disorder consists of recollection phenomena, a numbed emotional responsiveness, and signs and symptoms suggestive of hyperawareness and anxiety, with a tendency for everyday occurrences to act as reminders of the old trauma, resulting in an unpleasant flood of panic feelings.

School failure may result from an increase in their anxiety and agitation that develops after repeated assaults. A sudden deterioration in performance may occur. However, it is important to note that some children may respond in a paradoxical way in school and become overachievers in their drive to overcome their personal secret. The first-class student who is a good athlete – surely he cannot be a child sexual-abuse victim? It is known that such an adaptation to repeated stress can occur (Rutter, 1985), and many case histories attest to it.

Follow-up studies indicate that those children who were victimised at the youngest age and involved for the longest period of time, and where the severity of the abuse was greatest, are likely to show more severe psychological sequelae (Browne & Finkelhor, 1986). However, it is probable that a variety of other factors, such as parental emotional unavailability, neglect, physical abuse, and involvement in pornography, play a very important role when one considers the psychological effects upon a child. In addition, the effect of the intervention of the helping professions along with the legal response (see "The effect of the intervention system", below) may make significant contributions to the overall impact.

In summary, the majority of sexually abused children demonstrate behavioural or emotional consequences in the wake of discovery of their plight. A minority are not so affected, at least in the short term, although we do not know what happens to this group later on. The effects are likely to be modified by many other factors to do with the surrounding family or care system, and the co-existence of other noxious influences on the child. There are no specific behavioural or emotional effects which prove that the child has been sexually abused, only those which raise the possibility of CSA along with other explanations, to the professional.

Victim psychology

The psychological adaptation of the child sexual-abuse victim in response to continued abuse is a key factor in appreciating the current psychological status of the child to be interviewed (Summit, 1983). The developmental process of becoming a victim is a complex one. When we are evaluating a child shortly after disclosure, it is relatively easy to forget the long process of adaptation that all family members will have gone through before the current time. The chemistry within the family necessary for abuse to occur starts early, long before the child is actually sexually misused. In intrafamilial sexual abuse, various family patterns are possible. Sometimes the child and future abuser are emotionally close to each other. Gradually the abuser sexualises the contact between them (grooming). In other respects the abuser may be relatively emotionally available, yet paradoxically misusing the child. In other situations the abuser's relationship with the child may be hostile or rejecting, months or years prior to sexual aggression coming into the picture. If the child has another care-giver, he or she may be protective or alternatively not so, in either of the above two situations. In any event, perhaps because of a problem within the abuser himself, and/or because of his inability to form normal and satisfying adult relationships, combined often with a weakening of the usual taboos and restraints against sex between an adult and a child, the sexual abuse itself starts (Finkelhor, 1984). The sexual misuse may start with excessive physical contact, followed by fondling, and perhaps oral sexual contact much later on. Typically, the contact gradually progresses to intercourse, but this is less common in the early stages. From the victim's perspective, the activity may not seem abusive to begin with, and this, combined with the close relationship that may exist with the abuser, may be very confusing to the child. Younger children may think that perhaps all love and affection is similar to their experience and, furthermore, that this must happen to all children. In some part of themselves, victims often report feeling that it was somehow wrong, but at the same time not wishing to lose the emotional warmth they experienced when they were with the abuser, despite the high cost.

The child's cooperation at this stage is obtained by this gradual distortion of the care-giver/child intimacy. Perhaps the child will be told, "don't tell your mother or she will get ill", or "this must be our special secret", or "if you tell, you will end up in a children's home, and never see your mother again", or "no one will believe you." Overt threats of physical harm are often not necessary, and the misuse of parental authority suffices to keep most children silent. However, sometimes the threats are violent and threats of death or mutilation of either the child or someone whom the child loves are used to ensure secrecy (Lister, 1982). Sometimes gifts and special favours accompany the threats, with the promise of a special position within the family for the child if the secret is kept. The feelings described by victims combine a mixture of fear, sexual stirring, and perhaps most of all the desire to be loved and attended to (Berliner & Conte, 1990).

By this stage in the evolution of the victim's experience, the child's sexual feelings will have been harnessed and exploited by the abuser. The child's innate sexuality and normal responsiveness to sexual stimulation is often encouraged and developed by the abuser. The abuser frequently develops and uses his knowledge about the child's potential to respond sexually to his actions, finally rendering the child an accomplice to his own abuse. This process is a subtle one and frequently seen after a period of exploitative interaction between abuser and child. Not surprisingly, it is one of the most difficult processes to untangle and make sense of after CSA has been discovered, both for victims (Jones, 1986) and abusers (Conte *et al*, 1989). The child now feels equally responsible along with the abuser, and it becomes even more difficult to tell anyone about his plight. Such children's self-image is a very negative one, and to confirm just how 'bad' they really are, they seem to take great pains to have their negative self-image reinforced at every opportunity. For example, they will reject praise, and search instead for punishment as negative reinforcement from adults. It is not surprising, then, that by adolescence, they have turned to numerous antisocial activities.

When a professional person, or perhaps a foster parent, first comes across a child who is at the end of this long-term adaptation, they often see a very unappealing child. Interviewing the child or young person in this unfortunate state of adaptation will, therefore, be very difficult, but perhaps an appreciation of the child's biography and an understanding of how they have survived, can help make these young victims more understandable.

The victims may show features of a post-traumatic stress disorder (see above). However, in the case of intrafamilial sexual abuse, the stressor is a repeatedly occurring one. Hence, the victim may be reduced to a state of continual high anxiety which may be combined, paradoxically, with a state of inaction and a relatively frozen ability to create any change in her situation. Shengold (1967) has described this process very poignantly, and used the concept of a "rat person" to describe the effects of such prolonged overstimulation and abnormal stress. Peterson & Seligman (1983), from a somewhat different conceptual point of view, first of all studied the effects upon animals of subjecting them to overwhelming and relentless stress from which there was no escape. They termed the result of such prolonged and repeated stress 'learned helplessness'. Sometimes the professional onlooker may not be able to understand this process, and may disbelieve and respond with anger towards the human victim who has not protested more effectively. Such professional response is well recorded in the fields of spouse abuse (Pizzey, 1974) and in adult rape as well as in the child-abuse field (Tyler & Brassard, 1984).

After the disclosure has been made by the victims, the guilt connected with their participation in the abuse may intensify over the ensuing months. The feelings of guilt and personal responsibility may become combined with feelings of loss, and grieving for the emotional warmth that the abuser provided. At that stage, it is difficult for the victim to appreciate that the warmth and emotional availability were only provided at a price. The victims begin to feel that they caused the family's break-up, and perhaps the incarceration of the abuser. Retraction may be a frequent accompaniment at this stage (Summit, 1983).

The effect of the intervention system

In addition to the factors associated with the incest itself, there remain secondary effects of the system's response to the disclosure of the abuse. Included within these are the potentially negative effects of multiple interviews with the child, insensitively performed medical examinations, prolonged foster-care placement with subsequent disruption of family bonds, accusatory investigative styles which alienate the child's carers, and the break-up of the family. To these may be added the harmful pressure of repeated court appearances, frequently accompanied by delays and postponements. It has been recognised in many areas that the system's response does not have to be so cumbersome and inflexible, and coordinated treatment-orientated ways of responding to the disclosure of a child's sexual abuse have been designed. Giarretto (1976) pioneered such a programme, and others have also been developed. It has been suggested that the emotional distress that may be caused by some of the above secondary influences is lessened by this type of system response. One of the purposes of this book is to contribute to the reduction of distress when children who have suffered trauma need to be examined psychologically.

This chapter has summarised important aspects of the knowledge base within the fields of sexual abuse, family violence and victim psychology, which are essential understanding for the practitioner interviewing children where CSA is suspected. We can see that sexual abuse is a diverse phenomenon and that a thorough appreciation of the predicament of the sexually abused child is a necessary prerequisite for the practitioner. We shall next consider the contribution of psychological research to the field of interviewing children in this area.

2 The contribution of psychological research

The children's interviewer has to appreciate the developmental status of the child. This may be easy to dictate, but hard to achieve, for there are many theories available. An adherence to one particular school of thought without consideration of its critics or the contribution of other perspectives can blind one to the abilities of the individual child. Similarly, an absence of understanding about the differences in the capability of children of different ages can be a major handicap to the interviewer. There are good introductions to the topic of developmental psychology (see McGurk, 1975; Donaldson, 1978; Mussen *et al*, 1984) as well as critical, comparative reviews (e.g. Gelman, 1978). Most of the available theories of how children's minds develop describe how most children perform the majority of the time. They are useful general frameworks for appreciating an individual child, but there are certain limitations. For example, in the search for pattern and similarity, the differences between individuals can be lost. For this reason, any theory of the stages that children are said to negotiate while they grow up has to be paralleled by a knowledge of individual differences (see Kirby & Radford, 1976). There is not only a difference between persons, but also differences within the same child from one day to another to be taken into consideration when interviewing. Hence theoretical frameworks that include psychological and social development can be useful, practical guides for what to expect of a child at a given age, provided they are used flexibly.

These general considerations should inform our interviewing approach and enable us to make use of some of the specific areas of research inquiry that are relevant to interviewing sexually abused children. They include children's memory and suggestibility, their knowledge of the anatomy and function of sexual organs, and the study of children as witnesses to traumatic events. These specific areas are now considered in more detail.

Children's memory

This section refers to some of the findings of psychological research on a child's memory and its development through the child's life. A good introduction to the psychology of memory can be found in Brown *et al* (1983). Full reviews of the subject are available (e.g. Perlmutter, 1980). An excellent compilation of the major research findings in the area of children's memory and its application to children's ability to recall and relate that which they have experienced, is to be found in the book edited by Ceci *et al* (1987*b*). Briefer reviews which summarise the salient aspects for our field of concern include those by Davies *et al* (1986) and Goodman & Clarke-Stewart (1990). From this area of research and inquiry, there emerge several themes which have practical importance for clinical interviews with children who may have been abused.

Over the last 10 years, we have realised that memory is not a unitary phenomenon akin to a video-tape residing somewhere in the depth of a human being's brain, which, if only connected to the appropriate machine, can be successfully accessed. It is now generally accepted that no such tape recording exists, and that 'memory' consists of many elements that together comprise the overall idea of a memory. Instead of remembering a particular event as a single memory trace, we remember a series of fragments, which we piece together when we are required to recall and relate an event from the past. Furthermore, the memory itself is not a static phenomenon, but a process that is subject to change, dependent upon the circumstances under which a memory is initially created, and upon the psychological state of the individual during the period following the event itself.

Along with the somewhat rigid views of memory development that used to be in vogue, there was also the view that a child's memory progressed from a nil capability to an adult capability, which was regarded as the best available. Again, we now think that this was a simplistic model and, in fact, different facets of the process which we call memory develop at different rates. The poorer capability of children freely to recall events in detail is due to their lesser experience and understanding about the world in general and to the inept ways in which adults attempt to gain access to children's memories, as well as because of their insufficient grasp of language (Loftus & Davies, 1984). However, children may do better than adults in some memory tests. A study in 1947 (Allport & Postman) illustrates this very well. A group of adults and children were shown a film of a subway scene in which a black and a white man were engaged in a fight. In the scene, it was a white man who was menacing by holding a razor. Children, if they recalled this detail of the scene, did not confuse the colour of the man who was holding the razor – they correctly reported it was the white man. Adults viewing the same scene often erroneously reported that it was the black man wielding the razor. This study suggested that as human beings grow older they acquire an increasing number of prejudices that may actually affect how they perceive and remember the world that they live in. It also emphasises that the development of memory from infancy to adulthood should not be seen as a gradual achievement of the capability of adulthood. We should emphasise just which parts of memory develop, and which parts become more reliable, and which less reliable, with increasing age.

Another very interesting finding has been that young children who experienced events that made an impact upon them, even before they were able to speak, remembered those events accurately when they were 3 or 4 years old, and used their current language to relate the facts. This phenomenon even occurs without any rehearsal occurring between the time of the event and the moment when they recalled the event and related it to their parents (Todd & Perlmutter, 1980).

It is well known that the more time that has elapsed since an event was experienced, the less a person can recall about that event. This 'forgetting curve' occurs in both adults and children and in itself emphasises how important are the early statements that children or adults make soon after an event is experienced. In children, it has often been assumed that this process occurs to a greater extent than in adults. However, such research as we have suggests that the long-term capacity of children to remember past events is as good as that of adults. In experimental situations with children the effect of time does seem to cause some memories to be susceptible to suggestion (Goodman & Clarke-Stewart, 1990).

What about the amount that a child recalls compared with an adult? In general, it is agreed that children recall less detail about any particular event than do their adult counterparts, and that this capacity gradually increases as children grow older. Thus, by the age of 10 or 12, children can become as adept as adults at remembering prior events. However, there are anomalies. For example, if elementary-school-age children and adults are compared on the quantity that they can recall on subject matter that they are very familiar with, then if anything children do better than adults (Lindberg, 1980). It does appear, however, that children below the age of 5 recall less detail than do older children or adults (Goodman & Helgeson, 1985). As has been noted, children, in general, recall less because their understanding of the world in general is not so well developed at earlier ages, and also because they may not have a sufficient grasp of language to be able to relate the events.

Children are often considered to have a problem putting events in the order in which they actually occurred. However, there is good evidence that, for events of central importance to children, their capacity to place events correctly in temporal order is surprisingly well developed, even for very young children (Gelman, 1979).

We know that the stress and personal impact of an event has an effect upon the memory process. We can distinguish between those events that have a personal poignancy for the child, and ones that may be considered a peripheral experience from the child's point of view. Central events are better recalled at a later date than are peripheral ones. (In this regard, peripheral events to the child may be very 'central' as far as the investigating adult is concerned and *vice versa*.) Clinical experience (Pynoos & Eth, 1984; Jones & Krugman, 1986) emphasises how important the personal impact of an event is on one's capacity to remember it. In addition, the added impact of the various pressures that bear upon the child, that were described in Chapter 1, have to be taken into account. Sometimes children may take months before they are able to relate a traumatic event that they experienced, simply because of the fear and terror that causes them to suppress their memory (Lister, 1982; Summit, 1983; Russell, 1986).

Both adults and children may be suggestible, and their memories thereby distorted in the stage when they are retrieving their memory and recalling it for an interviewer. In both adults and children, the memory that is most susceptible to this alteration is that which is of less central importance or personal poignancy to the subject. Children, probably more than adults, are influenced potentially by the authority of the interviewer, and this implies that clinical interviewers should be careful not to overemphasise their authority in relation to children when they are interviewing them. Young children (3–4-year-olds) were shown to be more resilient to misleading questions about abuse if they were interviewed without undue authority (Goodman & Clarke-Stewart, 1990). Lastly, the suggestibility of an individual can be assessed in the clinical situation, as has been reported in individual case studies (Gudjonsson & Gunn, 1982; Jones & Krugman, 1986).

It is not uncommon to hear the view expressed that children are not able to distinguish between what really happened in objective reality and what happened in their dreams or thoughts. They are said to confuse fact and fantasy in this manner. The often observed capacity for young children to relate the events of their dreams as though they were fact is quoted as an example. However, children's dreams usually have the hallmark of fantasy about them, and can be easily related either to events in the child's experience or imagery that they have seen on a TV screen, etc. Johnson & Foley (1984) have reported on their experimental findings in investigating this very question. In general, these results and others indicate that young children may indeed have problems distinguishing their own thoughts and dreams from what actually did happen, but only in a specific way. That is, children do not appear to be more likely to confuse what they have dreamed of doing with what they actually saw; on the other hand, young children do have problems distinguishing between what they have actually done and what they have thought of doing. Thus, the idea that there is a generalised confusion in children between fact and fantasy does not have much support in the experimental literature, but, in certain areas, children do show a relative inability to discriminate fact from fantasy. From the point of view of the courtroom, however, it is unlikely that a child will have a problem distinguishing what happened from their thoughts or dreams. On the other hand, they may report that they actually did something, when in fact they only dreamed or imagined that they had done so. It is of interest that children subjected to severe trauma will sometimes claim that they struck or defended themselves against the onslaught of their attacker, when in fact they wished and dreamed that they had done so, but had not been able to do so in reality (Terr, 1979; Pynoos & Eth, 1984).

Can children identify a face from memory? Photo-identification line-up is an accepted part of police investigations, but is not used very often in psychological investigations with children suffering from trauma. When exposed briefly to a person who is threatening, both adults and children do not identify their aggressor from a photo line-up with 100% accuracy. Reasons for this include the deleterious effect of stress upon their memory, the 'gun focus' effect, the effects of race upon face-recognition, and the influence of preconceived notions upon retrieval (Loftus & Davies, 1984). It seems, from the research that has been done, that children do as well as adults at this task after the age of approximately 6 years. However, most of the experiments that have been conducted have not tested the influence of the extended contact normally involved in a sexual assault on a child. In the experimental situation, 3-year-olds in one study (Goodman & Helgeson, 1985) had a less well developed ability to identify a face accurately in a photo-identification line-up, than did 6-year-old children. In a study by Marin *et al* (1979), younger children were less inclined, however, to make false identification in a line-up experiment than were their adult counterparts. In an individual case study where a child was forcibly abducted and sexually abused, and then an attempt was made upon her life, the 3-year-old child made an accurate, unfaltering recognition of the face of her aggressor from a photo line-up (Jones & Krugman, 1986).

All the experimental studies have underlined the harm that can be done by leading techniques in the questioning of children. What are the possible distortions in children's memory? (See Loftus & Davies, 1984; Goodman & Helgeson, 1985; Ceci *et al*, 1987*b*.) First of all, various types of inquiry can be considered leading. A question may be plainly leading to the child, for example, where did Daddy hurt you? Or, it may contain a bias towards one particular response as opposed to another, for example, Daddy hurt you, didn't he? Further, the interviewer may use authority inappropriately, thereby intimidating the child and leading him to respond to the authority rather than the question itself. Additionally, the question may include a preconceived notion of the interviewer; for example, because this child has been sexually abused, she must have been told not to tell, leading to the question, did Daddy tell you not to tell? Relentless probing for detail has been shown to produce error (Dent, 1982; Moston, 1990). Research has shown that these types of questions do negatively affect the accuracy of the reply (Dale *et al*, 1978; King & Yuille, 1987). They affect the younger child even more than older ones. However, research has also shown that events of central importance to the child are much more robust and difficult to distort in the experimental situation. This leaves the practitioner with a dilemma, because events recalled after employing leading questions may have really occurred, or alternatively may have been distorted by the manner of questioning. Furthermore, after distortion, adults and children tend to persist with their now distorted memory, making future clarification exceptionally difficult (Loftus & Davies, 1984), although not impossible (Ceci *et al*, 1987*a*; Zaragoza, 1987). We are, therefore, left with a problem of what to do when clinical circumstances imply the need to discover, but the child is silent. To go no further in questioning means to return the child to possible danger. While this is difficult for clinicians and the police, it may be better to accept that not all children will talk, than to use leading questions only to realise later that the veracity of the information gathered is difficult to assess. Occasionally, leading questions are necessary, but only after open-ended questions have revealed no information. In this latter circumstance, it is the potential for harm to the child should abuse not be disclosed that should guide the decision as to whether to use leading questions. Less suggestible forms of leading questions are available and can be shown to reduce potential distortion compared with more strongly worded leading questions. Dale *et al* (1978) have provided an example of this: ''did you see . . .?'' is more leading than ''did you see a . . . ?'' which is, in turn, more leading than ''were there any . . . ?''

Researchers have examined children's secrecy in experimental situations (see Pipe & Goodman, 1991). As practitioners in the field would guess, when children were told not to tell, especially by a parent, they tended to conceal information, fearing repercussions, even in the face of careful questioning.

All these findings have implications for how best to access children's memories. Some of these have been put to experimental test (Price, 1984). In this experiment, researchers employed the use of props and cues to young children's memory, and showed that the amount and accuracy of events recalled improves dramatically when appropriate props are available to the child. Examples of such props include small dolls' houses with figures, cars, aeroplanes, and toys, that may resemble those of their everyday experiences. Furthermore, the availability of props that may be similar to those involved in the incident of abuse can be helpful, and anatomically correct dolls are an example of such an aid. Lastly, there is good evidence that returning a child to the original context in which he was abused can significantly improve the accuracy and amount of information recalled. Naturally, this cannot always be done, because of potential emotional trauma to the child, but if it can be, then it may be a very useful aid to a child's memory. There is no evidence that using aids such as the above in any way distorts the child's memory, provided that leading questioning is avoided when presenting such props and cues.

Children's knowledge of sex

There have not been many studies of normal children's knowledge about sexual anatomy and physiology at different ages (see Rutter, 1980; Melton *et al*, 1981; Waterman, 1986; Jones & Thompson, 1991, for reviews). Children of elementary-school age, and younger, may have a poorly developed concept of their own sexual organs, and an even greater ignorance about those of the opposite sex. Studies have not so far discriminated those children who come from families with a more open approach to sexual education from those not so exposed. Additionally, the influence of factors such as the degree of personal nudity that is permitted in a household, and the presence of siblings of the opposite sex, have not been correlated with what an individual child at a certain age may know about sexual organs and how they work. Girls may have no language or concepts to enable them to discriminate between their urethral and vaginal areas during elementary-school years. They may only have a vague concept of penetration, even if it was a feature of their sexual abuse. It appears that pressure upon the vaginal introitus creates the feeling of penetration in girls under the age of approximately 7 years, even when vaginal penetration has not occurred. In a similar vein, up to the age of 10 years, children may have quite bizarre ideas about the origin of babies (Moore & Kendall, 1971). Some children have a fear of pregnancy following oral sexual contact with an adult, and their concern will need to be clarified by the interviewer. Ejaculation is beyond the comprehension of young children, who may describe it as "Daddy peed on me" or "yucky stuff came out". The paradox of the adolescent incest victim who, although tragically 'educated' to the point of full intercourse, is woefully ignorant about sexuality in general, is one that has struck many workers in this field (Porter *et al*, 1982).

There has been surprisingly little work done on 'normal touching' within families. Rosenfeld *et al* (1986) looked at patterns of behaviour in middle- and upper-middle-class families in California. They showed that some genital looking and touching occurred between adults and children in the majority of families. The touching was usually accidental, and in the context of bathing and dressing and normal family intimacy.

The child as a witness

There is conflicting opinion in the legal and psychological professions concerning how well children perform on the witness stand. There is also varied opinion as to whether children are harmed by testifying in open court, or whether it may prove a helpful vindicating process for the child to go through. It is probable that some children are helped psychologically by this public, authoritative vindication of their original statement (Berliner & Barbieri, 1984). On the other hand, there are other children who are psychologically harmed by the process of testifying. Both the issue of how well children do as witnesses, and that of the emotional trauma upon the child witness if he does testify, have been reviewed by Goodman (1984) and Flin (1990). We have studied sexually abused children who attended a criminal court to give evidence, comparing them with similar children who did not attend court. The results suggest that attendance at court is accompanied by greater psychological ill effect over and above the impact of sexual abuse itself (Goodman & Jones, 1988). These effects are greater if the child gives evidence repeatedly, lacks maternal support, or is providing uncorroborated testimony.

3 Preliminary considerations

General principles

The over-riding general principle is that of open-mindedness. We are not interviewing sexually abused children, but children who *may* have been sexually abused. Even when the level of suspicion is high, the interviewer has to maintain an open mind as to his or her professional conclusion until findings have been interpreted and the process of validation gone through (Chapter 6).

Great care must be taken to remain open and honest throughout the interviewing process as in any constructive, supportive interaction with children. The style of this relationship may be quite different from the usual experience of the abused child with adults and can pave the way for future intervention. Although it is a natural tendency to attempt to protect children from pain and disappointment, it will harm them if they are told that "everything will be okay, don't worry". The child will quickly see through this, and see no reason to trust another person in what may well have been a long line of disappointing adults. As well as openness, it is important not to make promises that one cannot keep, and the child should not be prevented from knowing about the next steps. The child must know that a variety of circumstances may develop as a consequence of the interview, but that no guarantees can be made as to the outcome. Such consequences may be continued interviews, interviews with other adults, possible foster placements, etc.

Flexibility to change direction should be incorporated into the 'style' of the interviewer, so that allowance can be made for the child's special needs. There is no 'cookery book' of predictable questions and answers, nor a particular order in which they would be put. However, in every interview, there are specific content areas that have to be covered. These areas will vary from case to case. Prior to the session, the interviewer can delineate clear goals, which may be made into a check-list as an *aide-mémoire*. However, the child needs to unfold the details of the story at her own pace. This is a critical point, as often the interviewer is under a great deal of pressure to gather information needed to substantiate criminal charges or secure the child's safety. The interview should proceed at the child's tempo, and not that dictated by the pressures of the 'system'. The more pressured the child feels, the less the interviewer will learn. Leading questions must be avoided. This particularly applies to questions about specific sexual acts and the identity of alleged perpetrators. The most dangerous situation is where the entire tenor and approach of the practitioner is to suggest a certain set of answers, for example, through using suggestions and leading questions which leave the child without any alternative but to agree to the interviewer's agenda. It follows that interview approaches which facilitate reluctant children have to be used skilfully and with care.

The interviewer must be willing to accept the possibility that the first interview may not result in any information at all, or may involve a child who is not willing to share any information and refuses to speak. An inability to substantiate clearly, or dismiss, an allegation of sexual abuse should not be taken as an outright failure. The clinician has to accept the fact that not every interview goes as planned. In some cases, further interviews will be necessary. Some may continue after a short break of a few minutes or hours; others may reconvene after several days. However, when deciding whether to undertake another interview, the balance between the potential for harm through repeat interviews, and the degree of professional suspicion that the child may be being harmed through abuse, have to be carefully weighed. The interviewer has to ensure that a personal sense of having 'failed' to discover what, if anything, has occurred to the child is not obscuring the balancing of these opposing harms. In the UK, the Child Protection Court (Family Proceedings Court) has the power to restrict the number of interviews with the child (Jones, 1991). Similarly, the Memorandum of Good Practice for interviewing children in criminal cases cautions against conducting more than one interview with the child unless there is a good reason for doing so (Home Office, 1992).

Personal aspects

Interviewing sexually abused children can evoke strong emotional reactions within the professional. Sexually abused children are often keenly attuned to these responses and feelings of adults, and may more quickly perceive the interviewer's disgust or sadness. Thus, the child may adapt her behaviour in the interview to lessen the reactions of adults, or may close up completely in order to avoid revealing emotion. As mental-health professionals, we like to think of ourselves as open, problem-free facilitators, but may have to face the possibility that a child victim's account of sexual abuse may resonate some personal well buried memories. If this is the case, there should be no shame attached to requesting that a colleague interview in one's place. Contemplation of such team support within an agency is critical if such openness is accepted. Feelings of horror, disgust, anger, and fear are commonplace. However, morbid curiosity is seldom discussed. The extreme of this interest may actually give the interviewer some type of vicarious reaction. How we deal with these and other feelings is a personal matter, but it would be folly to ignore them. We must be aware that such feelings can exist, and may affect a case's outcome if not taken into account. Thus, it is essential that an interviewer ponder these aspects of style, personal openness, and flexibility, as well as psychological factors, in pursuing a role as interviewer of sexually abused children. Further, caution must be given not to arrive eagerly at the issues of the investigation prematurely, or to succumb to the pressures of the system too readily. Such overenthusiasm tends to hamper the child's development of confidence in the interviewer and can lead to secondary distress. The interviewer must enter the session with an open mind and lack of bias; a 'don't yet know' stance (Goodwin *et al*, 1982) is critical if one is to gather important data that have such an impact on a child's future. Leading questions can lessen the usefulness of the interview when presented in court and affect the entire process of evaluation, but may also discourage the child's spontaneity and ability to trust the interviewer. Awareness of all these factors has to be incorporated into each interviewer's style.

Not every social worker, mental-health professional, medical practitioner, or police officer should expect to be proficient in the interviewing of children. Advanced knowledge of child development and psychological dynamics is required to interview these children accurately and skilfully. Professionals who are 'child-orientated' can reasonably develop these techniques, but many skilled clinicians are simply not adept at interviewing all sexually abused children. Some interviewers may be very understanding and knowledgeable with school-age children, but may be left helpless in the presence of a 3-year-old. These variations in skill are to be expected, and taken into consideration when assigning personnel to such projects. Variety within a cultural context must not be overlooked, as the interviewer has to understand the range of behaviour that is culturally accepted and practised.

There has been much deliberation as to whether the child victim should be interviewed by an adult of the same sex, by an adult of opposite sex to the alleged perpetrator, or by a male–female team. Unless the child's history is known prior to the interview, it may not be possible to arrange this for the child. In any case, the child's reaction to the interviewer may provide helpful information, and should be recorded. Clearly, if the child is visibly frightened or extremely agitated in the presence of a particular sex, every effort should be made to replace the interviewer with someone with whom the child is more comfortable. Clinically it seems that the issue of the sex of the interviewer may be a more important factor with teenagers.

The setting

The choice of the setting for the interview may vary according to the urgency involved in a case and the availability of resources, as well as the nature of the allegations. In any case, the atmosphere in which the interview takes place is as critical as who conducts the interview. A playroom or space that is familiar to the child is preferable, but not always available. The interviewer can adapt many settings to enhance the child's comfort by creating a childlike atmosphere that incorporates the use of certain props, toys, and art materials. The combination of setting and materials helps to elicit verbalised accounts of abuse, as well as to provide an arena in which to observe the child's play. (For very young children, it is useful, if possible, to conduct the interview in the place where the abuse is alleged to have occurred.) The itinerant interviewer may carry a bag of such materials that can be used in a variety of settings. Suggested materials are listed in Appendix A.

Prior information

Access to prior records and history may prove helpful to the interviewer. It is best to know all the details available if an allegation has been made. This will often consist of a statement that a child has made to a friend or trusted adult. Basic information about the family is useful as well as some details of the child's everyday life, so that a starting point for the interview can be made. Additionally, what terms the child uses to describe body parts and sexual function, and any family names or terms of endearment that the child has for significant persons in his life should be discovered. Lastly, the family's style with respect to personal nudity, bathing, viewing sexually explicit material on video or in magazines, etc., should be explored. All this provides an important backdrop of information upon which to proceed with the interview. Having done this, the interviewer can note important information as an *aide-mémoire* to be taken into the session with the child.

Consent

When a standard mental-health assessment of a child is being conducted, parental consent is considered to be given implicitly. Such an assessment may well include screening questions concerning the possibility of abuse and trauma, including sexual maltreatment. Typical examples of such situations include the assessment of children whose symptoms raise suspicion of CSA, for example, teenagers who have overdosed or self-mutilated. If a professional decides that a more facilitative approach is going to be needed during the interview (such as that outlined in Chapter 5), then, ideally, parental consent should be sought. However, this may pose many practical difficulties if the parents themselves are directly or indirectly involved in the abuse of their child. Great care has to be exercised to avoid exposing the child to inordinate pressure from care-giving adults if full consent is sought in this way. If there is any doubt that consent will be forthcoming, or if it is refused, despite strong suspicion that CSA is a possibility, then the child's situation should be rapidly discussed with the local social-services department. There should not be a delay between the request for consent to the interview and the evaluation itself. If there is, inordinate parental pressure may be placed on the child to keep her silent. A child who is in care, or a ward of court, will require the consent of the local authority, or of the court, respectively (see Jones, 1991, for effect of recent legislation). If the mental-health professional is in doubt, then the advice of the appropriate defence organisation will need to be sought as a matter of urgency. Difficulties such as those indicated above do occur, but often direct discussion with the parents about the need for a proper interview with the child will be accepted, and consent forthcoming. We generally try to obtain the assent of the child as well as formal consent from parent or guardian. We take a very similar approach with respect to consent about the method of recording the interview (e.g. audio- or video-taping).

Presence of parents

A common question asked is whether a parent or significant adult should be present. Consideration must be given as well to other persons who may be called on for further information, or who may need to be present for legal purposes. The child, obviously, is affected by numerous interviews, so that care must be given to eliminate the re-questioning and prolonged steps often present in such investigations. Generally, if the child is given easy access to the parent, and if the interviewer can see the child casually, with the parent, prior to the session, the child will feel comfortable enough to separate from the parent and talk with the interviewer alone. This author often shows the child where the parents will be waiting, and gives the child full permission to find them if necessary.

There may be unforeseen problems if a parent is present. The parent may appear to be supportive and non-abusive, but at the start of the interview the parents' standpoint is unknown. We have seen so-called non-abusive parents become experts at non-verbally reminding the child to keep the secret while saying "tell the truth". Therefore, while the interviewer is in the stage of not fully understanding either child or family, it is best to see the child alone, if at all possible. If the parent must be present, then he must sit to one side, and be instructed not to help, nor to express his feelings or fears.

The only preparation that most children require is minimal, and along the lines that they are going to talk with 'X' about some things in the family. Specific preparation is best discouraged so as to avoid the child being coached, or his anxiety being elevated unnecessarily.

Recording the session

Documentation and recording of the interview can be done with a variety of methods; available resources and agency requirements affect the choice. Though often distracting to the child as well as to the interviewer, some note-taking is required to describe the process. Audio recording obviates the necessity for extensive note-taking, but has to be complemented by written comments describing the child's non-verbal behaviour. Video recording provides the most complete form of record. Video recordings can be very helpful for the clinician, enabling him or her to review the interview at a later date. Video is not a panacea however (MacFarlane, 1985). Without first-class equipment, sound and picture clarity may leave much to be desired. Additionally, there are implications for confidentiality, and for storage of tapes. It is generally considered that the tapes are potentially subject to laws of discovery, and therefore have to be stored and not erased, in case there is future legal action. Clinicians have to consider if the use of video-tape is likely to reduce spontaneity or even frighten the child. Those making video records primarily for the purpose of availability for court purposes should liaise with the local Crown Prosecution Service in order to discuss format, storage, and the labelling requirements, as well as aspects of interview style. Consent and assent should be sought before video recording. In the USA, video-taped recordings have proved to be a frequent catalyst to positive legal decisions on behalf of children, by offering evidence that is difficult to articulate secondhand. The use of video-tapes has lessened the necessity for children to be subject to repeated interviews, and appears also to have reduced the need for the child to give evidence in court.

What sort of interview?

Different professionals approach CSA with separate professional responsibilities. Thus, the police are concerned primarily with crime detection, although they are likely to be concerned also with child safety and protection. The social-services department is mainly concerned with child protection and safety, and whether such safety has to be secured through court orders. Psychiatrists and psychologists are concerned with the influence of sexual abuse upon the child's development. General medical practitioners, paediatricians, and health visitors are similarly concerned, but may also be involved with assessing the child's physical growth and development, as well as any physical abnormalities associated with sexual abuse. All these professionals come across children who might have been, or are currently being, sexually abused.

From the professionals' perspective the first consideration is to be clear about their role in relation to laws and local procedures for reporting abuse concerns. Hence cases of high suspicion will need to be referred to the appropriate professional for an investigative interview, together with accompanying assessments (see Chapter 5). On the other hand, there will be many occasions when a child either makes a spontaneous comment during the course of one's professional work, or the professional will have grown suspicious that the child in question may have been sexually abused. If this suspicion is of significant degree then the professional will doubtless refer to the mandated agency for a full-scale investigation. However, there are a great many other cases where suspicion is of a much milder order and is entertained by the professional along with many other possible noxious influences which may be affecting the child's development. Only mild suspicion of this kind should not automatically be referred to mandated agencies. Such a course of action would be unlikely to be good for the child, who in any case may well respond with silence to such precipitous action. In addition, if the child has just begun to make the possibility of CSA known to the professional within a relationship of trust, referral to a mandated agency may be positively harmful. Professionals who are not members of mandated investigation teams therefore do have to sift and sort their concerns to decide whether the appropriate action is to refer on, take no further action or alternatively monitor and follow up the child themselves, until the situation is more clear. It is for the latter professionals that the next chapter is written, to suggest screening approaches which fall short of full-scale interviewing.

4 Screening for the possibility of sexual abuse

In many instances suspicion of CSA is relatively slight, but the implications were the professional to confirm suspicion are disproportionately high. Hence professionals are concerned that if the child is being sexually abused this should be discovered as soon as possible and the child protected. On the other hand, investigation is a disruptive process which should not be initiated unless sufficient suspicion of CSA exists in the first place. CSA usually occurs within a context of secrecy, adding a further complication to the assessment of suspicion. Professionals react differently to these pressures: some eagerly suspect abuse in all troubled children, others prefer to avert their gaze (Ounsted & Lynch, 1976). Retaining a balanced perspective can be difficult in such circumstances.

Principles and overall approach to screening

The most important principle is to keep the line of communication open with the child, without raising alarm or anxiety prematurely. Wherever possible, and where appropriate, a parallel attempt to keep the line of communication open with the parent or care-giver will be necessary too. The professional may well have to contain his or her own anxiety about the possibility of CSA, maintaining a vigilance over a period of time and holding back from referring the child on until suspicion is sufficient to warrant an investigation. In order to do this it is helpful to discuss the risk to the child with other colleagues and seek consultation outside one's immediate colleagues.

It may be possible to identify adults in the child's world who are likely to be trusted and with whom the child can develop sufficient confidence to enable him to unburden himself. These adults may be professionals or carers. If the child drops further hints suggesting the possibility of sexual abuse, these identified adults can then listen and respond appropriately. Specific concerns may have been raised by referers, parents, or the child, which should permit further discussion, play, or the unburdening of concerns and worries by the child. Much depends upon the type of professional contact as to what kinds of activities can reasonably be explored. Thus general discussion about sleeping and bathing arrangements, privacy, discipline in the home, the application of creams and medications or other worries and concerns that the child may have about particular people or places can often take place. This can be done in a way which permits the child to express concern and allows her time to express any problems which she has. It can be argued that these approaches are part and parcel of many professional consultations. It is probable that the professional's ability to convey acceptance and interest, together with an ability to listen to personal concerns without shock, are just as important as the specific inquiry approaches suggested above. Nevertheless, the timely use of such phrases as "do you have any other worries about that?" enable suspicion to be explored further.

Particular types of professional consultation may allow for the possibility of CSA to be explored in different ways. For example, child psychiatric and psychological assessments may, through the exploration of the content of areas of mental pain or anguish, permit pain about CSA to be disclosed. Similarly, while a child is being examined by a paediatrician, the reason for particular signs and symptoms can lead to the discovery of sexual abuse. (See below for further detail.)

With older children the professional may be asked to discuss directly the consequences of disclosing sexual abuse, as the child develops the courage necessary to unburden the secret. The author has often found himself discussing the consequences of disclosure in the most general way before a young person has decided to disclose any specifics concerning abuse. As with the full-scale investigative interview (Chapter 5), professionals have to be prepared for a negative outcome to their screening attempts. This may be because there is nothing untoward to disclose, or because the child is simply unable or unwilling to discuss abuse. Sometimes, as professionals, we simply do not know.

Medical practitioners such as general practitioners and paediatricians may well be able to make use of the consultation to enable the suspicion of sexual abuse to be explored further. For example, during an examination of the child's genital area she can be asked "how did you get sore down here?" A more specific question would be "has anyone touched you or played games with you down here?" It may be helpful to have the parent situated behind the child's head, out of the child's direct view when such a question is being posed. If the doctor is more suspicious because of what the child is reported to have said, behavioural difficulties, or aspects of family functioning, the doctor may be in a position to say to the child "it's hard to talk about things if your Mummy [or Daddy] is here isn't it?", continuing to ask the child if perhaps he would like his mother to be outside just for a moment. If the doctor is male, a female nurse or receptionist may need to come into the room at this stage. We have found that parents will sometimes respond to an open approach such as this.

A further approach which can sometimes be useful involves going through the differential diagnosis for the physical complaint which is arousing the suspicion of sexual abuse. This can be done directly with the parent but keeping the child within hearing distance. The differential diagnosis is directed towards the parent in a matter of fact way for the complaint, such as repeated urinary-tract infection with no clear cause or repeated vulval or penile soreness without explanation. The possibilities of infection, allergy, masturbation and molestation are listed. With some children it may be possible to involve them in this discussion of diagnostic possibilities. An approach such as this will be appropriate only where a doctor is relatively confident about the quality of the parent/child relationship and considers that inappropriate pressure on the child will not result from diagnostic possibilities being raised.

In some circumstances the doctor continues to be concerned but without sufficient clinical evidence to warrant a referral to the mandated child protection services. It may be possible then to say to the child, ''who would you tell if you did have a worry?'' In this way discussion about trusted adults can occur without providing a leading question about any specific area of concern.

In other professional settings screening approaches may also be possible. For example in child mental health settings children can be asked directly about the nature of their concerns and anxieties and the things that they are upset or sad about. Open-ended prompts can enable children to talk about matters such as sexual abuse, if this is their concern. For example: ''Anything else you haven't been able to tell someone about (that you'd like to tell me)?'' ''Anything else been happening that you can't tell anyone about?''

If the level of suspicion of CSA is moderately high, some of the lines of inquiry outlined in Chapter 5, inquiring about sexual abuse directly, will be justified for the mental health professional to use. For example: ''Has anyone hurt you or perhaps touched you in a way that you didn't like?'' The climate has changed considerably in child psychiatric circles, so that inquiring about sexual abuse is no longer considered inappropriate. Lanktree *et al* (1991) found that in their study of children in a general child psychiatric clinic the proportion of positive reports of child sexual abuse increased from 7% before children were screened about the possibility, to 31% when child psychiatry team members were trained to ask a few screening questions about the possibility of sexual abuse.

The consequences of screening

Professionals will be left with several possible options having screened for the possibility of sexual abuse. Firstly, there is no further action. Secondly, continue to monitor and follow up the child and family keeping the options open. Thirdly, there can be referral of the case for a full investigation into the possibility of sexual abuse when suspicion is converted into a definite possibility of abuse. A further possibility will involve seeking advice and consultation from a specialist in the field to clarify the way forward. Whatever decision the professional makes it will usually be necessary to discuss the action taken with other professionals who may be involved with the child's care. This will be especially important if the suspicion is more than mild, because the summation of the concerns of several different professionals involved with the same child and family may make the way forward much more clear. In the UK the process for achieving this would be through a case conference or planning meeting. Whatever path is taken by the individual professional, the inquiry and decision making should be carefully recorded, in whatever way is appropriate and available, so that it can form part of the child's record. If suspicion becomes a real possibility and in turn a probability, the process by which the sexual abuse was discovered will be very important, both legally and clinically. Thus records, even of the briefest screening approach, constitute an important aspect of good practice.

Investigation or assessment interviews

In Chapter 5 the full-scale investigative interview is described. The purpose of such an interview is to discover whether abuse has happened, in as much detail as is possible to achieve. A distinction must be made between such an investigative interview and an assessment of a child by a mental health professional to discover the extent, if any, of psychological ill effects on the child as a consequence of abuse. The concern in the latter situation will be to discover what effect abuse, and its context, has had upon the child's mental state and psychological functioning. Such an assessment will be needed in order to plan a comprehensive intervention. The assessment of the child in these circumstances will be part of a wider assessment of the child and family context, and will have a historical perspective to it (Department of Health, 1988; Adcock *et al*, 1991). Generally speaking, child mental health professionals do not interview 'well' children, who are free from disturbance, in order to see if they have been abused. Social workers and police officers, by contrast, do interview psychologically well children in order to see if the child requires protection or if a crime has been committed. Thus there are clear differences between assessment interviews directed at determining the state of mind of the child, and investigative interviews to see if abuse has occurred. Child mental health professionals may become involved in the investigative process when very young children, or children with learning disabilities, or children who are overtly disturbed are involved. In such cases a child mental health perspective to the investigation is necessary (Royal College of Psychiatrists, 1988).

We return now to the investigative interview, having discussed approaches towards lower degrees of suspicion.

5 The interview itself

Those who engage in the challenge of interviewing sexually abused children develop their own techniques over time, and choose to develop a certain 'style' and structure within the interview itself. The support of a team or colleagues within an agency or department is essential. Supervision and/or consultation is a must, not only as the clinician starts in the area of sexual abuse, but throughout his or her career. Many who have tried to continue in this field without these emotional and professional supports have become less effective over time.

Structure of the interview

There is a range of opinion within the field concerning whether or not the interview should be structured, and if it should, to what extent. At the one extreme, there are proponents of a rigidly pre-planned format (e.g. White *et al*, 1986). In these and similar protocols, the child is steered back 'on track' if he or she strays from the planned format. The interview described here has a specific aim and purpose (that of discovering if CSA has occurred or not) and has a series of phases to it, but its precise flow and format is adapted to the individual child. Additionally, the choice of materials used to help facilitate the session is based upon clinical judgement and those materials chosen are tailored to the individual. For example, a 'talking' interview may be used with one child, the use of dolls and toys with another, similarly aged, child.

The series of phases is as follows:

(a) gaining rapport
(b) initial inquiry about sexual abuse
(c) facilitation
(d) gathering specific detail
(e) the closing phase.

Not all child interviews need all the phases. In addition, the order may well vary from child to child. However, for ease of instruction and description, the above format is used to describe the process. Some specific issues, for example, leading questions and the use and misuse of anatomically correct dolls, are discussed in the text. There are certain sections of a typical interview which do require pre-planning. Thus the interviewer is recommended to memorise a mental 'check-list' of items to be covered during the phase of the interview where detail is gathered. Additionally, it is helpful to have rehearsed a pre-planned approach to the use of degrees of facilitation prior to interviewing dependent on case information available. Also, those professionals who are just starting to interview children may find it useful to have a few rehearsed introductory inquiry phrases ready for use and/or a pre-planned approach to the closing phase, so that they do not become lost for words or forget the need to close a session in a humane way for a child. However, preparation of this kind is quite different to the cookery-book approach to interviewing (King & Yuille, 1987). The structure presented here is intended as a guide and by way of an example only.

Most published approaches on this topic agree on the need for a graded approach, with gradually increasing specificity to the inquiry process. Table 1 compares the phases outlined in this schedule with those in the Memorandum of Good Practice (Home Office, 1992) in order to orientate the reader and allow cross-reference.

TABLE 1
Comparison of interview phases

This schedule	Memorandum (Home Office, 1992)
(a) Gaining rapport	I. Rapport
(b) Inquiring about sexual abuse	II. Free narrative account
	III. Questioning:
	A. Open ended
	B. Specific yet non-leading
(c) Facilitation	C. Closed questions
	D. Leading questions
(d) Gathering detail	IV. Closing the interview
(e) Closing phase	

(a) Gaining rapport

The main aims of this phase of the interview are to establish a relationship with the child, to engage the child's interest, and to make an assessment of the child's level of understanding. In order to establish the relationship, as in other interviews with children, the practitioner concentrates on neutral aspects of the child's life, such as school or friendships. It may be possible to talk about how they travelled to the interview, or any interests that they have such as sports or television programmes. Normally, one talks about the child's home, but this may be inadvisable if the child has fears or negative emotions attached to talking about home. In general, specific matters, especially to do with sexual abuse, are avoided at an early stage in the interview. It is sometimes important to avoid drawing out the preliminaries for too long a time, particularly with adolescents, who will sometimes become bored. One girl remarked, after several minutes of what she perceived as small talk, "When are we going to talk about IT?"

As part of this phase of gaining rapport, the interviewer can explain who he is and describe his role. This should be brief and should avoid reference to the question of sexual abuse. The interviewer should avoid identifying himself as someone who protects children or ensures that children are safe, etc. The interviewer might make brief reference to the way in which the suspicion of sexual abuse has emerged (see below). Thus if the child has said something suggestive of sexual abuse (the most common presentation) the interviewer can make brief reference to this without being specific about the content.

There is no place during any phase of the investigating interview for teaching children about the 'correct' words for sexual organs, personal safety, nor for lectures about what it is that adults should and should not do. The aim of the interview is simply to find out if anything of a sexually inappropriate nature has happened, and if so exactly what that was.

Acknowledgement of the difficulty of such a session may be given in an empathic or non-intrusive manner at any stage during the interview, in order to build rapport with the child. During the interview, we may need to pause and reflect upon such a difficulty, letting the child know that she will not be pushed, prodded, or coerced into surrendering information. We want the child to know and feel that she has given her assent to the process, as well as the consent that may well have been obtained from parents or guardians. The interviewer's anxiety to discover if the child has been abused can result in too eager an approach, confounding the result and raising the child's anxiety.

At some stage during the session, but not necessarily in the first phase, the issue of confidentiality of information may well arise. This gives the interviewer the opportunity to tell the child who will be told the results of the interview. The interviewer must avoid promising confidentiality if it cannot be assured. Paradoxically, most children will respond to this approach even if they initially seek total secrecy with the interviewer.

The rapport phase may be a suitable time to give the child permission to answer "don't know" in reply to any direct questions. The Memorandum of Good Practice (Home Office, 1992) also recommends that if it is considered that the interview should contain a section where the child is reminded of the importance to tell the truth, it should be done during this phase and not later in the interview.

Through these means the interviewer will have established a working assessment of the child's level of understanding and will be able to judge what complexity of language will be appropriate during the rest of the session.

(b) Initial inquiry about sexual abuse

It can be difficult to move from the phase of gaining a rapport to inquiring about possible sexual abuse. In general the first steps in this phase will be aimed towards encouraging the child to provide a spontaneous account about any sexual abuse to which he has been subjected. The interviewer will need to be careful to avoid altering her demeanour and style at this point, as this would raise the child's anxiety. Sometimes, children are aware of the reasons for the interview session and want to talk about their experience. The slightest prompt may enable them to give a spontaneous account. The child may well start to talk in response to the interviewer identifying herself, or while explaining the reason for the interview session. If not, it is still possible to encourage free narrative.

One method is through asking the child why she thinks she has come to the interview. Another route is through the interviewer making use of the way in which the possibility of sexual abuse was first presented for professional attention. The interviewer's line of inquiry will depend upon the type of suspicion that has led to the current investigation. Broadly there are four categories: (i) something the child has said; (ii) an adult's suspicion about a place or person; (iii) physical disease; (iv) the child's behaviour. Initial inquiry questions are guided by the type of suspicion. Typical approaches might be as follows:

(i) Something the child has said.

"I have spoken with X, and it sounds as though a lot of things have been happening in your family. Can you tell me a little bit about that?"

"You told me that you were talking with me today because someone in your family did something that he shouldn't have* – can you tell me a little more about that?"
[*Substitute here whatever it was the child said when answering why she thought the interview was taking place (see "Gaining rapport", above).]

"Your mummy said you had talked to her about some things that had upset you – can you tell me about that?"

(ii) Adult suspicion about a place or person.

"X told me that you don't like it when Uncle John comes to stay at your house – can you tell me about that?"

"Tell me who looks after you when your mum goes out . . . . What things do you like to do with (babysitter) . . . . Anything that you don't like doing with (babysitter)?"

(iii) Physical disease. In cases where there is a physical disease or condition which has raised the suspicion of CSA, the child can be asked if he knows how he has become unwell, or how he got sore. A spontaneous account may follow a line of inquiry about what led to the child going to the doctor's, etc.

Children who have been physically abused or investigated because of neglect may well fall into one of the above groups. They should also be asked if anyone has hurt them in any other way, once it has been established that they have been suffering from a type of maltreatment other than sexual abuse.

(iv) Behaviour. Behaviour change or type (e.g. sexualised behaviour) may raise suspicion of CSA. There may be no other clues, such as those above, to allow a lead into initial inquiry. Raising concerns about CSA may then be quite difficult for the interviewer to do without being fairly direct. Possible approaches are:

(1) Inquiry about the child's symptoms (anxiety, depression, nightmares), for example:

"Tell me about the things you've been worrying about."

"What happens in your scary dreams?"

"When you were playing like that with Fred, . . . have there ever been any other times when you've played games like that?"

"Has anyone ever played games like that with you?"

(2) General inquiry about family, or friends. Here it is possible to use a family drawing to discover who the child likes and/or dislikes, and for what reasons.

During these attempts to encourage the child's free narrative the interviewer's style is encouraging and reassuring, giving the child as much time as is needed so that she does not feel rushed or pressured. It may well be appropriate to acknowledge the child's difficulty or reticence. Gentle acknowledgement along the lines of "Did anything else happen?" or "Tell me a bit more about that, can you?", as well as merely reflecting on what the child may have said is the style of this phase of the interview.

In some situations these approaches will have been sufficient to encourage the child's spontaneous recall of abusive events. If this has occurred the practitioner will not require the more facilitative approaches described below. However, not infrequently, there is a need for more clarity about whether or not sexual abuse has occurred, and in all likelihood the most likely source of information is the child. Hence the interviewer, while still remaining open minded, will need to employ more facilitative approaches.

(c) Facilitation

In this phase of the interview, the practitioner follows the route through which the suspicion of sexual abuse has arisen, as before, but with more enabling techniques. The approach involves a combination of aspects of style, the types of questions used and, with younger children, the availability of toys and play materials. The essence of the style is relaxed, yet purposeful. The focus is gently maintained on the matter under investigation without any sense of pressure. The interviewer takes care to avoid being too intrusive, avoiding excessive eye-to-eye fixation, or inappropriate touching of the child. The interviewer aims to create an atmosphere of acceptance and safety throughout. Interestingly, experimental studies of error production in children have begun to highlight the relevance of these issues of style and general manner (Dent, 1982; Tully & Cahill, 1984; King & Yuille, 1987). It may well turn out, after further research, that these issues of style will prove even more relevant to a likelihood that the child will make errors of recall than the type of questions *per se*. In the author's view, a further aspect of interviewer style which is relevant is to avoid showing embarrassment, disgust, shock, or aversion. Similarly, the interviewer should avoid vicarious interest in the subject matter (children have said to us ''all he wanted was to hear what my dad did . . . he seemed to get turned on by it, so I shut up . . . wasn't going to tell him anything''). The interviewer will often need to attenuate his emotional responses, while at the same time demonstrate an appropriate degree of warmth and a genuine empathy for the child's predicament.

Facilitative questioning

Questions in this phase become increasingly more encouraging, leaving the most suggestive or leading questions to the last (if they are employed at all). It is recommended that overtly leading questions, about detailed sexual acts or specific perpetrators of such, are rarely used, if at all. None the less, between the extremes of the encouragement of free narrative and the overt leading questions are several approaches to questioning which, if used with care, can be very helpful for the child, while not distoring the child's recall. Questions can be phrased in a permission-giving or enabling way. Objective or direct questions may be posed to the child. Questions such as these provide a mild-to-moderate degree of facilitation, depending on the context or style in which they are used. Some examples are as follows:

"Your Mummy said that you had some worries about being touched on private parts of your body – can you tell me a bit more about that?"

"Has any one touched you on your body in ways that made you feel uncomfortable?"

"Has anyone touched the private parts of your body – like where your swimsuit goes – and made you feel uncomfortable?"

"Did anyone, even a grown-up who you are close to, ever touch the private parts of your body, like where your swimsuit goes?"

(Direct questions)

"I talk to a lot of children and sometimes to children who have been touched on private parts of their bodies. It can help to talk about things like that. Has anything like that ever happened to you?"

"Some kids are touched in private places on their body by people who are close to them, like someone in their family who they know very well. Has anything like that ever happened to you?"

(Permission-giving and ending with a direct question)

Questions such as these avoid suggesting to the child a particular person as a possible abuser. On the other hand, if one were to ask, "Did Daddy touch you . . . ?", the result could be highly misleading.

"If Daddy had touched you on your pee-pee, how would that have felt?"

(Hypothetical)

Sometimes the either/or format is useful, but usually only after the child has indicated something and subsequently become stuck for words. The hypothetical format is not used for specific acts or persons, except very rarely, because of the problems of subsequent interpretation. Even if the answer is affirmative, one is still left wondering if maltreatment has taken place or if the question has suggested the answer (see "Leading questions", below). The format may be helpful in enabling the child who has already disclosed something during the interview, but has then become too fearful to proceed to talk (Leventhal *et al*, 1987). Hypothetical questions may also be of value when enabling the child to talk about fear, etc., for example, "If you did have a secret, who could you tell about it?"

Other questioning styles can be facilitating, especially those that reduce the child's anxiety. For example, circular questioning is a useful approach. In this method, the interviewer talks around and around the focus of the question, dwelling on items that do not elevate anxiety, with a style that is anxiety-reducing. Then, at an opportune moment, an aspect of CSA is inquired about.

If the child says yes to facilitative styles of questioning such as those in the examples above, the question which follows needs to be put in an open-ended style. For example, if the child replies "yes" to any of the above questions, then the next question should be along the lines of "Could you tell me a bit more about that?".

Language

There are certain 'dos' and 'don'ts' with respect to language used in the interview. It is preferable to use the child's own terms for sexuality and sexual organs (see pages 16–17). 'Why' questions are generally avoided, as they are confusing for the child. The interviewer's 'why' questions are likely to be interpreted by a sexually abused child as imputing guilt, for example "Why didn't you ask for help sooner?" "Why did he do that to you?", etc.

Sentences should be kept short, specific questions should only contain one idea, and double questions avoided. Questions containing a double negative seem to be especially confusing to children. Pronouns are better kept to a minimum, and names used in their place; for example, "Did Daddy do anything else?" is preferable to "Did he do anything else?"

Leading questions

The issue of leading questions is a controversial one in this field, as assessment interviews may lead to the filing of criminal charges and civil court actions to protect the child. A leading question is one which suggests the required answer, or contains assumptions which the child has not previously alluded to (Home Office, 1992). Generally speaking, the use of such questions should be avoided. They are not so contentious when directed towards matters unconnected with the possibility of abuse. Also, with very young children or those with learning difficulties, some degree of leading may be necessary to enable the child to talk at all (Home Office, 1992). These caveats notwithstanding, it is important to avoid leading questions about a particular offence, or to suggest that a particular person may be responsible for it. These are guiding principles for interviewers concerning leading questions (Home Office, 1992).

The issue of leading questions is not straightforward. The degree of suggestion in a question and the interviewer's style and use of authority all have a bearing on how damaging a leading question is. First, there is a clear relationship between the degree to which the question is subjective (thereby potentially leading the child to an answer already suggested by the interviewer), and the subsequent distortion of memory and recall. Both research and clinical experience attest to this. Those suggestions made by the interviewer which employ maximum use of authority, and contain questions such as "Did Daddy touch you here?", are particularly troublesome compared with those recommended in the section above. Second, the timing of the subjective question (potentially leading) has to be examined. The questions that precede and follow the subjective question are of great importance. In the sequence recommended, initial questions are open-ended, with subsequent ones becoming more specific during the course of the interview, until, finally, a subjective question might be used, for example "some kids are touched. . .". If the child says "yes", the next question should be open-ended. If the child's subsequent answer merely recapitulates the suggestion inherent in the subjective question, only limited conclusions can be drawn. However, if the child goes on to describe detailed sexual acts with specificity and emotion, we can be much more confident that the answer is the child's and not based on the interviewer's question. Third, there is a major difference between an interview which contains one or two leading questions, and one which contains nothing but leading questions. The latter has been aptly described as a 'driven' interview.

In fact, in experimental situations and within clinical experience, children are remarkably resistant to leading questions, provided that the atmosphere of the session and the interviewer's manner permits the child to disagree or to say "I don't know". In clinical experience, the most difficult situations are where leading questions are part of an oppressive, relentless atmosphere within the session to "get the disclosure" (Jones, 1989). It is the latter type of session which has understandably received criticism from the judiciary in recent judgements.

Dealing with fear

Children who have been sexually abused are usually required by the abuser to keep silent about their experience. The corollary that all secretive, silent children are sexually abused is not the case. Hence, the approach to the reticent, fearful child who appears to be hiding something, must be open minded. Such a child may be hiding an abuse secret, or may be concealing another unknown concern. Not all silent children are 'in denial' or 'not yet disclosing', but some are. How can we help the abused children to reveal their secret while avoiding inappropriate suggestion and influence to the non-abused? Some general principles are described in this section, and specific methods that may be helpful are outlined in the following section.

If children show signs of fear, sadness, or guilt, one must acknowledge that and attempt to empathise with them. The child should be asked if he feels uncomfortable, and then discussion with him about how clarifying what has happened will help him in the end, even if it causes difficulty in the short term, should take place. (It should not be promised, however, that all will be well if they are able to talk about their abuse, because in reality matters may become worse in the short term.) Acknowledging that it is hard to talk can be facilitating with a reticent child. Asking the child what he is scared about can relieve anxiety in a similar fashion.

It is often more productive, when the child is showing signs of resistance, to return at intervals to the traumatic subject throughout the course of the interview, rather than pursuing the sexual-abuse theme relentlessly.

Free play is an important element of the interview, especially with younger children, and can be very helpful with fearful youngsters. Periods of free play may occur at any time during the session. The author's preference is to avoid pre-planning a set period of free play, and instead to have episodes of free play with the dolls' house, drawing materials, or larger dolls, throughout the interview. Some practitioners recommend a period of play without the interviewer present, at the end of their session (e.g. Jampole & Weber, 1987).

Direct gaze fixation is often too intrusive for children, and various techniques are described below that include within their benefits the factor of avoiding eye-to-eye gaze. In the following section, different techniques are described which have been found helpful in eliciting detail. These have the advantage of using materials familiar to the child, and they are methods through which children can show or illustrate to us their concerns. These techniques reduce the sense of intrusion and help the child to relax. The most intrusive style imaginable is that of two chairs facing each other, with the interviewer and child in close proximity. If one adds to this scene an authoritarian manner and an insistence upon verbal communication solely, many children will remain silent or, even worse, produce unreliable answers (Goodman, 1984).

Similarly, **touch** may carry ambiguous implications for a sexually abused child. Even a well intentioned, comforting gesture can be interpreted by the child as threatening, or alternatively, provocative. Therefore, an interviewer should exercise great caution before incorporating physical contact into the interview.

Use of toys and play materials

The following techniques are suggested as useful ways to encourage a child to discuss any abuse that may have occurred. These techniques may also be useful methods to supplement and elicit further detail once a child has said that she was sexually abused.

Small figures, with accompanying dolls' houses, and small cars, are useful props with which children suffering from trauma can indicate their experience (see Appendix A). Once a child begins to play with these figures, he may be gently encouraged to talk about his play. Joining with the child while avoiding overintrusion is a key issue at this stage. If premature identification of the figures and actors is demanded by the interviewer, the child may well leave that particular play scene and embark upon another one. Children may also relabel the characters during the course of a play sequence and say what they are doing out loud, and if this occurs, they should be permitted

Fig. 1. A 7-year-old girl's sexualised drawing of her father; detail of ''his penis'' at the right

Fig. 2. A child's self-portrait

Fig. 3. A sexually abused girl's drawing of her family

to do so. Here again, the essence of the approach is to help children expand upon their play, while avoiding directing it, if at all possible.

Puppets (both glove and face) may be used to re-enact situations that the child has difficulty recalling with words alone. If, for example, the child is getting stuck, then one can say that "it is difficult to talk isn't it", and that sometimes it is easier for him if he can talk through a puppet figure. Once he gets the idea that he can talk through a puppet figure, then instead of the puppet talking to the interviewer, it may be easier for the child to have his puppet talk to the one which the interviewer holds. In this way, the conversation can become less threatening to the child. With puppets and with similar techniques, where the child uses play to represent real life, we need to bring the child from the allegorical towards talking in the first person about actual experiences.

Larger dolls, between 12 and 18 inches long, can be useful props to enable children to describe where and how they were abused (Britton & O'Keefe, 1991). They can also be useful to help indicate how the perpetrator approached and touched them. Ordinary, commercially available dolls are perfectly adequate for this purpose, and have the advantage of avoiding the contention of anatomical dolls.

Art is widely employed by many evaluators (Stember, 1980; Goodwin, 1982; Naitore, 1982). The child may be asked to draw himself, or perhaps his family doing something together (kinetic family drawing), or may be asked to draw siblings. Some evaluators encourage children to draw the alleged perpetrator also. When using art in this way, flexibility becomes very important, and a variety of media can be used. For example, some children enjoy using clay or Play doh®, and can sculpt their experience for the interviewer. These techniques can be very useful with children who do not want to talk about the experience, or are feeling very reticent. Having the interviewer and the child involved in drawing or using clay alongside each other can be a useful technique and put the child at sufficient ease to disclose misuse. Winnicott (1971) used a somewhat similar process when interviewing children he saw for consultation on paediatric hospital wards, naming it the ''squiggle'' technique. With this method, he passed a rudimentary drawing first to the child and then the child would do one for him – each would then complete the drawing in the way that he wanted to, thereby allowing an element of free association to occur between the two of them.

When art is used in this way, children may express overtly sexualised themes in their drawing (Fig. 1). They then can be asked to talk about their drawing. Art may also illustrate how poorly the child feels about himself (Fig. 2). Family drawings may reveal important themes concerning the child's position within the family, her view of the role of other family members, and sometimes her sense of disappointment as to the emotional unavailability of parents. Figure 3 shows a family of three – a sexually abused girl and her father occupy the house while her mother is ''sleeping under the pond''. Drawing can be a useful technique to allow small children to indicate what part of their body was hurt or harmed. Figure 4 illustrates the use of this method with a 2-year-old child who was asked to show on the drawing where she had been molested. She had previously said that her

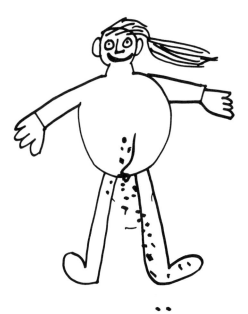

Fig. 4. A 2-year-old girl's indication of abuse

stepfather had hurt her and had pointed with her finger to her genitals. The child then became very reticent and the interviewer suggested that perhaps they could draw a picture of herself and her stepfather in order to help her. The interviewer then drew the little girl while she drew her stepfather on a separate piece of paper. Then, the girl moved across and made dots on the interviewer's drawing of herself, followed by a firm line drawn upwards from her crotch to indicate where she had been touched.

Line drawings can be useful to enable children to describe abuse. Simple line drawings can either be done by the interviewer or commercially available ones can be used for this purpose. In the past, interviewers have used publications about prevention of sexual abuse, designed to teach children about touching or strangers, as an aid to investigation. There are few, if any, advantages of this technique over those already described. In addition, there is the potential for suggestion to the child which may preclude the usefulness of these preventative materials for legal purposes. Furthermore, their use potentially confuses education about personal safety with investigation of possible sexual abuse. For these reasons the use of such publications is not recommended.

Sometimes, with an older child, picturing a traumatic event as though projected into the distance through a window, with both interviewer and child turned and looking out together, can be a useful technique. Milton Erickson used many methods similar to this to communicate with his patients (Haley, 1973).

Anatomically correct dolls

Despite the media and legal attention given to anatomically correct dolls, they are only one of several techniques used by most professionals investigating CSA allegations (Kendall-Tackett, 1992). The materials described above are much more commonly used by interviewers, yet not so systematically scrutinised as anatomically correct dolls. Various terms have been used to describe anatomically correct (AC) dolls (e.g. anatomically detailed, anatomically complete, sexually explicit). These dolls are rag dolls with genitalia, body hair, and bodily orifices all present. They are available in different racial styles, and some have tongues, fingers, and detachable body hair. There have been criticisms that the genitalia have been disproportionately large, but a recent study has demonstrated that their sexual parts are of average proportions (Bays, 1990) They are 'big business', as may be evidenced by the slick marketing on the stalls of some CSA conferences. All self-respecting agencies who interview children consider they must have at least one set. But are they necessary? In the author's view they can be useful in certain circumstances, but should not be the mainstay of all evaluative assessments of all young, potentially abused children. Clearly, with anatomically correct dolls, children can be more precise when indicating where they were misused, but such dolls may also be intrusive and somewhat frightening for some children.

Until recently, because there were only pilot studies on the actions of normal or non-abused children when playing with anatomically correct dolls (White *et al*, 1986; Jampole & Weber, 1987), there had to be caution in interpreting children's play with them. When a child appears to be indicating sexualised contact with anatomically correct dolls, they should be asked who the people are, and what is happening, etc. What the children do with the dolls can help augment their statements, but not too much weight should be placed on the play exclusively. Despite assertions to the contrary, there has been no convincing evidence to support the notion that AC dolls *per se* cause spurious accounts. Goodman & Aman (1990) tested the notion that the combination of AC dolls and suggestive questions was prone to error. Their careful design consisted of a group of children interviewed with AC dolls, another with ordinary dolls, and a third without any dolls. The 3-year-olds were more suggestible, overall, than the 5-year-olds, but the group with AC dolls did no worse than those interviewed without them. The 'AC-doll' group did not produce false or spurious reports. For the 5-year-olds, dolls of either sort produced better results than free recall.

There have been several studies of the play of young, non-abused children with AC dolls (e.g. Sivan *et al*, 1988; Glaser & Collins, 1989; Everson & Boat, 1990). One finding has been that few of the children exhibit sexualised play during the assessment. However, Everson & Boat (1990) demonstrate that within a subgroup of their sample who were poor, black, male, and aged over 5, rates of sexually explicit play with AC dolls were in excess of 20%. Thus there are probably large variations in how children, both abused and non-abused, may respond to AC dolls. Nevertheless, professionals tend to deduce a great deal from the free play of children with such dolls. There is, in addition, considerable individual and between-group variation in the interpretation by different groups of professionals of the meaning of children's play with these dolls (Boat & Everson, 1988).

At present, the best uses of AC dolls are with pre-verbal, and barely verbal children when asking them to demonstrate abuse, and to provide a further medium through which a child of any age can describe abuse if she has already done so by words or using a drawing. Additionally, if she has described abuse to the extent she is able, and shows a need to demonstrate further detail, the use of dolls may be indicated (e.g. Jones & Krugman, 1986). Even in these conditions, 'ordinary' dolls can be equally useful in most situations. It is not recommended that AC dolls be used as the initial, sole means of inquiry. It is suggested that a set of dolls be available, yet out of sight of the child, and that 'ordinary' rag dolls and dolls suitable for the school-aged child (see Appendix A) be used in preference to AC dolls.

If AC dolls *are* brought out for the child, something such as "These are dolls that look like people really look like underneath. . ." should be said. Whether the child spontaneously explores the doll should be noted. They should be used to encourage recall and speech, in preference to relying on the child demonstrating events remembered. The child should be permitted to change the identity of the doll as the interview progresses, and encouraged to talk about the doll without pressure, leaving plenty of time for free play. The child then becomes confident and at ease with the dolls. At this stage, a process of naming the doll's bodily parts may be gone through, after which the child is asked if anyone has touched him here (pointing to the doll's genital area). After this stage, more detail is requested, attempting always to encourage spontaneity in the child. The doll should not be named, "Let this be Daddy, etc.". By contrast, the child should be allowed to talk and demonstrate at her own pace. If the child has not already indicated who the doll represents, he may be asked "Is this doll like someone you know?" (NB, not, "Is this Daddy?"). If the child says "Daddy", more detail is requested (see "Gathering specific detail", below).

In summary, it has yet to be demonstrated that AC dolls help sexually abused children more than other, regular dolls. We do know that toys and materials in general help children to convey their memories accurately, but no convincing evidence exists for the superiority of AC dolls over other materials. By contrast they can cause confusion to professionals when interpreting the meaning of children's play. There is no evidence that they cause harm, though, *per se*, or abnormally sexualise the child, or are the source of major errors in recall. Professionals are generally poorly trained in their use and there is wide variability in the interpretation of findings from AC-doll interviews. For all these reasons this author does not recommend their use, certainly in the initial stages of an interview. They may be helpful to clarify accounts of CSA already given by a child, where specific detail is needed but other approaches (as in the sections above) have not proved fruitful.

Free play

Some authors recommend that a specific period of free play is incorporated into the interview with the young child (e.g. Vizard *et al*, 1987; Jampole & Weber, 1987). This period is useful in certain cases, if it is possible to incorporate it. Most of the authorities who recommend this phase are particularly concerned to observe the child's free play with AC dolls. Some sexually abused children re-enact or demonstrate sexual activities during free play, whereas the non-abused do so less frequently (Jampole & Weber, 1987; Glaser & Collins, 1989). However, as already noted in the section on AC dolls, this observation does not constitute a 'test' as to whether abuse has occurred.

In this interview approach, free play is generally interspersed, in small periods, throughout the session as a whole. There is a balance to be struck between free, unstructured play, and the purposeful focus on the investigation. Too much unstructured play can result in the child's anxiety increasing. On the other hand the child will sometimes seem to benefit from a 'rest' from the more focused approach. Generally, the author's experience has been that the change from one style to another for a definite phase of the interview is somewhat confusing to the child, and that it is preferable to adapt to the child's cues and vary the style of the session accordingly. This seems to be less disjointed as far as the child is concerned.

Behavioural observations

Direct observations of the child's behaviour and his use of play are critical and as important as the spoken material. (For good reviews of the range and meaning of children's play, see Tizard & Harvey, 1977; Garvey, 1977; Rosenblatt, 1980; Rubin *et al*, 1983.) Assessment of the effects of the abuse and of the experience itself cannot be done wholly by examination of content only, but should include the interpretation of the behaviour in the interview. The interviewer can document behavioural changes, mood shifts, etc., as they relate to subject matter. The following types of behaviour should be noted:

What is the change in mood? What topic caused the mood to change?
What topics precipitate a change in behaviour?
What topics distract the child?
What topics cause the child to make attempts to distract the interviewer?
What topics does the child avoid altogether?
What does the child's affect tell you? What does his body language tell you?
What play materials does the child choose? What does he avoid?
In general, how does the child cope with the anxiety of the interview?
How does the child interact with the interviewer? Is he appropriately distant, too friendly, etc.?
Does the child change grammatical tenses or pronouns, or use word substitutions?

These observations can be documented by taking notes or by reviewing a video-tape of the session. If audio-taping the session, these shifts in behaviour and affect need to be separately recorded, or the interviewer will lose those critical details. This is particularly relevant with young children who may be pre-verbal, or who choose to remain silent.

(d) Gathering specific detail

If the child has been given an account of CSA in outline, more details will often be required so as to lessen the need for further interviews. Following the child's lead by allowing her to give her story at her own pace, with her own words, is the key issue at this point. Caution should be exercised here to avoid the use of suggestion or any leading form of question, as the interviewer can become overanxious, and in her eagerness dampen the child's spontaneity. One has to be cautious to modulate one's own emotional response both in this way and with respect to the content and details which the child may relate. For example, one 5-year-old girl recanted her story quickly when she gauged the emotional response of her interviewer, and some weeks later said "I said it didn't happen, because she looked so sad". Sometimes the interviewer may be disgusted or horrified at the violence or perversity of the abuse that the child relates. We have to remain aware that abused children can be highly tuned to the emotions of others.

There are certain specific areas to be explored in addition to the details of the sexual abuse alone. To understand better the effects of the abuse on the child, to plan the appropriate intervention for the child and his family, and to provide the court with substantiating information, the interviewer should attempt to gather as much data as possible regarding the following areas:

What was the intent and emotion of the perpetrator?
Was there violence involved? Were any threats used? What were they?
   What were the words that the perpetrator used?
Where and when did the abuse take place?

Where and when are difficult for pre-school-age children, but connecting the abusive event to Christmas, birthdays, holidays, trips, or visits to special places, may help to clarify 'when'. Returning the child to the place where the abuse occurred may help establish which room was used, and more detail as to 'where'.

What did the child wear as clothing? Did the child dress up in adult clothing or use make-up?
How did the perpetrator gain the child's co-operation? What was the coercion or bribe?
Who was the perpetrator?

If the perpetrator was a relative or friend of the child, the child may be able to provide the adult's second name or other confirmatory identification. This is especially important, if the child says "Mummy" or "Daddy", in families where there is more than one person who is a parental figure for the child. If he was a stranger, the presence of identifying features such as a moustache, beard, or glasses should be inquired about. Young children can be helped in this by drawing the perpetrator and adding such detail.

Were there any other people present? Were there any other children involved? Did any other adults 'help' the perpetrator? Did anyone else ever do something like that to the child? Where were non-involved family members (parents or siblings) and what did they do?

Was there any blood present on the child's body? Did the perpetrator ejaculate?

Did the child or the adult(s) use any substances (i.e. alcohol or drugs), and if so, what? Sometimes children can draw the tablet that they were made to ingest in great detail, including the manufacturer's trademark.

Did the perpetrator involve the child in the production of pornography? Was the child shown pornographic material?

Did the perpetrator involve the child in acts of bestiality or sadistic ritual, or use sexual aids?

After the initial interview, the extent of the victim's participation in the abusive contacts will need to be explored. This is an important factor in the child's psychological adaptation after disclosure. It may be threatening to belabour this point during the first interview, as the child may already feel ashamed, guilty, or responsible for the abuse. Such psychological effects of victimisation will not necessarily be explored in an investigatory interview, but more probably in the ensuing evaluations for treatment.

The child may not spontaneously discuss any of these specific areas, yet the information is necessary to determine the child's immediate safety in the home, or to make visitation arrangements. The answer to some of these questions will help guide whether to interview siblings, who may have viewed the abuse or been privy to its existence.

(e) The closing phase

As the interview comes to an end, the child needs reassurance and vindication of the importance of the session. Direct congratulation is not appropriate, but to recap briefly with the child what he has talked about is in order. If the child has struggled to overcome guilty feelings, this should be acknowledged. One of the most important messages to convey is that the interviewer appreciates and recognises the emotional feeling and struggle that the child has been through during the interview. This recognition of the child's feelings is probably more important than 'pat' phrases such as, "It's not your fault".

The interviewer must prepare the child for what to expect in the future – continued interviews, psychological or developmental evaluation, possible treatment, etc. Predicting too far into the future should be avoided, however, and the interviewer should restrict herself to only describing the next step, especially as the future course of events cannot always be predicted and may only instil fear in the child instead of allaying anxiety.

The overall investigation/evaluation process can be discussed with the child, possibly eliminating some of the powerless feelings that she may have. Again, honesty and openness are the guiding principles here, and if one does not expect to see the child again, that must be directly explained to him before the end of the interview. It is extremely important to avoid making promises which cannot be kept.

Children of different ages

Reference to children of different ages has been made throughout the above, but some points relevant to specific age-groups are made here, in order to indicate areas which require particular emphasis.

The younger child (up to age 7)

The pre-school or young school-age child's speech and language development is immature, and non-verbal techniques will need to be stressed. Too many words will confuse the pre-school-age child, especially when he is asked to draw similarities, state differences between persons or events, or to sequence events in a linear time frame. With pre-school children, words such as 'tickle' or 'playing games' may be used instead of 'touch'. This is because, for very young children, the abuse may be confusing and seen as a game by them. Furthermore, phrases such as "hurt you", or "do bad things to you" should be avoided. Many children do not perceive sexual abuse in such a way and consequently will be confused by such notions. With the younger child, the recommended questions outlined when inquiring about sexual abuse cannot be asked out of the blue. Interviewer and child will need to develop an understanding between them as to what it is that is being addressed, so that the questions asked are not too complex for the child. There are various ways to do this by using the child's own lead and interest. Some methods are discussed in more detail (see "Use of toys and play materials" above). Drawings enable the child: (a) to know that we are talking about body parts; and (b) to identify and name those parts. After this has been established, a simple inquiry about sexual abuse can be made. Commercially available line drawings can be used for this purpose (Appendix B), or a body outline may be sketched on a piece of paper or on a blackboard and the child may join in the drawing. Occasionally, children will point to their own bodies. If this does happen, the child should be diverted from his own body to a drawing or doll figure in order to disclose further detail about sexual abuse. Similarly, dolls, whether anatomically correct or not, as well as other material such as clay, can be used to enable young children to focus upon the question of sexual abuse.

Pre-verbal children present even greater obstacles. The observation of free play then achieves greater significance, but great care must be taken not to overinterpret play. Children at age 1½–2½ years can sometimes respond to "Did X hurt you?" followed by demonstration on a doll or line drawing in response to "show me" (for an example, see Fig. 4). Additional parallel information from family and medical information may provide sufficient evidence of sexual abuse to warrant protection of the child. However, cases involving pre-verbal and barely verbal children are hard to substantiate at the present time. Unfortunately, paedophiles know this, and some choose young or handicapped children in order to avoid capture.

The primary-school-aged child (approximately aged 7–12)

During this age span, the starting phase is of special importance. This may be combined with a general assessment of mental status and psychological adjustment. During the course of the interview, time may be spent discussing the child's feelings, and the consequences of possible disclosure. This will often be necessary before the child will feel confident enough to entrust the interviewer with possible secrets. Art and drawing methods may be used during facilitation, but rarely anatomically correct dolls with this age group. 'Older' dolls, in male and female format, may be quite useful with this age group, as may anatomical drawings such as those by Groth (Appendix B).

Teenagers

With this age group, the question of the gender of the interviewer may be more important than with younger children. Once again, questions of privacy and the consequences of disclosure, as well as the confidentiality issues, may well need to be discussed with the youngster before she will feel comfortable discussing the sexual abuse. In general, the style of the interview with a teenager consists of using talking methods rather than play. Care should be taken to limit and control gaze fixation with teenagers to lessen the sense of intrusion and embarrassment that they frequently experience. Interviewer style becomes very important with this age group, confidence, acceptance, and a lack of embarrassment being important aspects. With a teenager, it should be recognised that he may well have developed a collusive partnership with an abuser over a long period of repeated abuse ('accommodation'; see Summit, 1983). Hence the need for great care with the questions and an acceptance of the teenager as a potentially complex victim. Similarly, the teenager, by this stage, may have abused other siblings or children in her care. The teenager will frequently resist the 'authority' of the interviewer, both because of her developmental stage and also possibly because of long-term intrafamilial abuse creating additional issues concerning authority. This may pose special problems during the interview, leading to the teenager asking the interviewer to justify why he *should* talk about it. In these circumstances the notion of 'should' is discouraged and the interviewer talks plainly and openly with the youngster about his predicament, the choices he faces, and recommendations for the best way out of the current predicament.

The interview in context

The interview described here is one part of a full-scale investigation (Kolvin *et al*, 1988). Other components might well include: family assessment, paediatric examination, investigations and questioning of alleged perpetrators, and sometimes psychological and child psychiatric assessments (Royal College of Psychiatrists, 1988). Only the interview with the child and the clinical process of validation (Chapter 6) are described here. Following the whole process of investigation there will need to follow a comprehensive assessment (Department of Health, 1988; Jones, 1991) of the potential for change (Adcock *et al*, 1991).

6 The process of validation

Once the interview has finished, the practitioner has to evaluate the outcome of the session, along with any other relevant information from the investigation, to decide if this is likely to be a case of sexual abuse or not. The issue is whether the case *convinces* the professional sufficiently for further action. 'Further action' ranges from discharging the case (if convinced that abuse has not taken place) through continuing the investigation or assessment (if uncertain), to child protection and/or initiating prosecution (if convinced). The truth or otherwise of the account is an ultimate matter and for the relevant court to make a finding upon. Social services, police and health professionals concentrate upon the degree to which the case is *convincing* to them. As professionals, we have no single or simple test of this. Instead we have to assess the data obtained from the individual case investigation in relation to what information does exist from the study of cases where sexual abuse has been confirmed or corroborated (e.g. through admissions, or through third-party witnesses). Regrettably, there is less systematic work of this kind than would be desirable. What follows is a personal approach to the clinical issue of validation. The basis is personal studies of cases which seem to be genuine or fictitious (Jones & McGraw, 1987; Jones & Seig, 1988) or a review of similar work by other clinicians (Goodwin *et al*, 1982; Sgroi *et al*, 1982; Undeutsch, 1982; Faller, 1984; Benedek & Schetky, 1985; Green, 1986) and reference to research literature where this is able to inform particular aspects of the validation process.

Sgroi *et al* (1982) have described their approach to validation, emphasising that the process centres upon a knowledge of the dynamics of child sexual abuse, good interviewing skills, and an ability to interpret the behaviour and physical signs obtained from the investigative interviewing. They break down the process of validation into the assessment of the child's behaviour, the results of the interview with the child, an assessment of credibility, the physical indicators of child sexual abuse, and finally the medical examination. Goodwin *et al* (1982) have similarly described their clinical practice that lessens the likelihood that a false report may be adjudged true. Faller (1984) has considered the question of validation and emphasises the importance of observing an emotional response consistent with the nature of the abuse, the presence of any idiosyncratic memories surrounding the sexual incident itself, the importance of the child's viewpoint of the event, his statements to other children, his play, and his abnormal knowledge of sexuality itself, as helpful elements in the process.

Heiman (1992) has reviewed the decision-making process in such cases and proposes that a multidimensional validation should include:

(a) the history of the symptoms
(b) the verbal account by the child
(c) phenomenology of abuse experience
(d) presentational style
(e) corroborating evidence.

The following approach to validation is suggested for practitioners. Primary importance is given to the account(s) of the child. Other information gathered from the investigation is considered in relation to this account. These other features either support or detract from the convincingness of the child's account. Thus broad areas examined when assessing the convincingness of the case are:

(a) the child's account and behaviour during interview
(b) the child's behaviour and emotional state (before and after investigation)
(c) the process of disclosure
(d) prior accounts or expressions of concern
(e) family
(f) physical and physiological evidence

Conte & Berliner (unpublished) have suggested that, in addition to approaches to validation based on items such as those above, consideration be given to the quality of practice used in the investigation. Were adequate standards employed in the initial investigation?

The approach set out below represents the items that have been found to be useful components of the clinical process of validation. They are not presented as definitive criteria for the assessment of the truthfulness of a report, but simply as a framework for making clinical decisions. The framework is intended to permit the clinician to assess the *degree of certainty* that can be applied to an individual case (Jones & McGraw, 1987; Jones & Seig, 1988; Kolvin *et al*, 1988).

The child's account

The account is examined for explicit detail of an alleged sexual abuse. Younger children, particularly under the age of 5 years, are not able to relate as much detail as are older children (Goodman & Helgeson, 1985). However, the more detail that is recalled, the more likely it is that the account refers to the child's own experience, especially if it is considered unlikely that an individual child can gain such detailed knowledge unless he had personal experience of the event in question.

The words and sentence formation should be congruent with the age and developmental status of the child; a 5-year-old child who falsely recanted her allegations, when asked why the sexual abuse had stopped some 18 months previously, said, "because it was inappropriate". This phrase belied its adult rather than child origins. As time passes, children do adopt their therapist's and case-workers' language, and so may appear unbelievable for this reason. When this is a problem, reference to the early statements of the child can help establish veracity.

The interview can be examined for signs of unique or distinguishing detail. This may be found both within the account of the sexual encounter and/or in unrelated recollections. Examples include children who describe smells and tastes associated with rectal, vaginal, or oral sex. One 4-year-old boy described a feeling of rectal stretching when being sodomised: "I felt like I wanna' go pooh pooh". Distinguishing detail may also be found in the description of the room or the clothes the child was wearing at the time. One 3-year-old girl said, "I had my panties on backwards".

The statement may be searched for evidence of a child's perspective of the abuse incident, in contrast to that of an adult or third-party. Such a 'child's eye view' of an alleged incident would seem especially hard to account for through coaching or adult interference.

The emotion expressed by the child during the interview is usually congruent with the events being described. A child may experience one part of the abuse as more offensive than another, but this differential may not coincide with the interviewer's assumption as to what was the worst experience for the child. The child may display signs of acute anxiety at key points in the interview, or the overt avoidance of particular areas of inquiry. Sexualised behaviour may be evident during the session. These and similar indications of emotional state tend to corroborate the verbal account. We may further ask whether the child's account is given in a rehearsed or packaged manner, or with appropriate emotion. Is the allegation delivered at the slightest cue from the interviewer, or in one or two sentences without the usual difficulty and reserve or hesitancy that children show? Is the emotion expressed genuinely experienced, or is it hollow in its manner of expression? Is the child bland, unemotive, and seemingly little perturbed by serious exploitation? While we would not expect all of these features to be evident in a single account, their presence or absence can be helpful in validation. Clues as to the child's psychological response to the abusive incident should also be sought. Did the child feel sad, frightened, angry, or guilty? Did she describe a remote or removed state of mind (dissociation)?

The pattern of the abuse described may help the practitioner, too. For instance, the clinical pattern in sexual abuse may not include intercourse, and may be restricted to oral or deviant sexual practices. In abuse by persons known to the child, it is common for there to be multiple incidents over time. A progression from fondling through oral sexual contact to intercourse over a period of months or years is common in incest cases. These aspects of the account involve comparing the nature of sexual abuse as described with the knowledge base from large case series.

The element of secrecy is usual and can be found in many accounts. "This must be our special game – don't tell anyone, not even your mom". Children may be coerced into activity, and/or threatened not to tell. They are frequently told that they will be physically harmed or removed from the people whom they love, if they do tell. Such coercion or threats are not always evident in the initial interviews if the child is too fearful.

There are other, less common features, which may help greatly in validation. They include descriptions of pornographic involvement, or sadism. These elements are probably under-recognised at present because we do not routinely inquire about them. Pornography may be present as part of the child's involvement in a sex ring (Burgess *et al*, 1984), or for consumption within the family only. One child described the ritual decapitation of a rabbit during her sexual abuse by a family friend, using the most graphic detail. The police were informed, searched the alleged perpetrator's basement, and discovered the dead animal, decapitated, just as the girl had described, along with other evidence of satanic ritual.

Associated features

The factors considered below provide support, or alternatively, if inconsistent, may raise doubts as to the veracity of the child's statement.

The child's behaviour during the period when she was being sexually abused may show some of the features associated with child sexual abuse (see Chapter 1). Whether the child being interviewed disclosed the abuse in a similar way to children in other confirmed cases should be considered (Conte & Berliner, 1988; Faller, 1990; Sorensen & Snow, 1991). Who did she tell, and what motivated her to do so? Is the disclosure understandable, given the pressures normally existing on children not to tell? Answering these questions can provide helpful information that may support or detract from the child's statement.

The child may have made a statement to other people before this interview. Often children talk to other children, or perhaps to neighbours, babysitters, or teachers, and the contents of their statements to these people may usefully be compared with the statement obtained from interview. The question of consistency between different statements made by a single child is more complicated than appears at first glance. There is usually, in truthful accounts, a consistency of the core elements of the child's exploitation, but there may be some variation in the more peripheral aspects of the child's story. Thus, the question of consistency is not an all-or-nothing matter. It may vary with the degree of personal poignancy of the particular experience for that child. Similarly, as stated above, the more violent elements of coercion and threatening behaviour by the perpetrator may be very frightening for the child, and consequently these elements may be suppressed by the child for a longer period than the sexual aspects of the abuse. This may give an air of apparent inconsistency to a child's account of sexual abuse over a period of weeks or months, but running through the account will be a consistent thread. In contrast to this situation, false statements are often made with monotonous consistency, and seem to show little sign of variation over time.

The way in which the child uses toys, playthings and drawing materials may be revealing. His drawings may contain highly sexualised themes, and his play with dolls may show similar preoccupations. His knowledge of sexual anatomy and function is often asynchronous with that of children of a similar age and social background. Other children who were involved or were perhaps in the household at the same time may have a viewpoint concerning the sexual abuse of the child being interviewed. Sometimes, they may have actually seen the abuse occurring, or at least have some knowledge of the activity. Sometimes the child who is being abused may have shared her secret with a brother or sister.

In those cases of abuse within the family, the biographies of other family members combined with the history of the family can provide helpful, supportive information. The alleged perpetrator's track record of violence, spouse abuse, alcohol and/or substance abuse, may suggest a type of individual who could be involved in sexual abuse of a child. The family may have a history of neglecting and abusing children, and may have sexually abused other children in the past. The history of their parental attachment and involvement with their children may provide further clues. An assessment may be possible as to the degree of dysfunction in the family, providing further data that may support or detract from the statement which the child has made.

Physical and physiological evidence

Physical findings suggestive of sexual abuse occur only in approximately one-third of cases (Royal College of Physicians, 1991). Three recent working parties have reviewed the available literature on physical signs in cases of suspected sexual abuse, providing helpful summary positions (Department of Health, 1988; American Academy of Pediatrics, 1991; Royal College of Physicians, 1991). There is a remarkable degree of consensus between the three. The Royal College of Physicians summarises the position, emphasising that many sexually abused children show no abnormal findings, that normative studies (of non-abused children), though scarce, do reveal a range of findings which could be confused with abuse, that examination techniques influence findings, that the dimensions of the hymenal and anal orifices may arouse suspicion, but signs such as tears in the genital area, pregnancy, sperm and blood enable the diagnosis of CSA to be made with more certainty. The College emphasises the importance of a full investigation and states that the single most important feature is the statement of the child (Royal College of Physicians, 1991).

Physiological correlates of truthfulness – such as the polygraph examination – suffer again from the same lack of rigorous testing, and so, while they might provide an indication, cannot be used with confidence as a measure of truthfulness.

Thus validation involves assessing as many of the above features as possible, in any single case, and weighing the relative weight of the individual elements. The emphasis should, however, be placed upon the child's statement itself.

Concluding remarks

Interviewing children who may have been sexually exploited requires a great deal from the professional in terms of a theoretical base and clinical knowledge. The application of these skills requires sensitivity to the needs of the individual child. For many children, successful application of these skills can mean relief from a veritable nightmare of misuse, thus beginning the slow process of repair and starting anew. If the initial interviews are conducted appropriately, the ensuing process will be more easily borne.

Appendix A

Suggested contents for an interviewing room

Necessary toys and play materials

Standard baby doll or rag doll – 12–14 inches tall – with crib (not anatomically correct)
Doll's clothes
Dolls suitable for elementary-school-aged children
Small dolls' house and furniture
Set of small doll figures – 3 inches tall – including family set, doctor-and-nurse set, police, and fire sets (last three are useful but not essential)
Open play car
Art materials: white paper, felt-tip pens, crayons.

Additional materials

Second dolls' house (useful for custody evaluations, foster-care placement, etc.)
Set of anatomically correct dolls
Plasticine, Play doh®, or clay
Toy telephones (two)
Police and/or ambulance play car
Tape recorder (audio)
Toy soldiers
Zoo animals
Puppets (set of humans – black and white)
Family face puppets
Animal puppets – glove variety
Picture books graded towards children of various ages including pictures of anatomy and body functions
Anatomical drawings (Appendix B).

Dressing–undressing puzzle by Galt Toys
The children's clothes are the puzzle pieces that lift out to show a nude boy and girl. The inlaid, wooden tray is brightly painted in non-toxic colours. 9½ × 12 in, 14 pieces.

Deluxe dolls' house family
Plastic, articulated figures with moveable head, arms, and legs. Their knees also bend, so the dolls may sit. These dolls are available from Fisher Price, only in the USA.

Playpeople
Plastic, moveable figures in a variety of costumes and settings with accompanying cars, buses and 'stage' settings for creative play. Child care, playground and hospital sets are available.

Most of these items are obtainable through local toy shops. Special resources to aid the interviewer are listed in Appendix B. Mail-order catalogues of educational toys are also available:

> Early Learning Centre,
> South Marston,
> Swindon SN3 4TJ
> (0793) 832832
>
> Hope Education Ltd,
> Orb Mill,
> Huddersfield Road,
> Waterhead,
> Oldham OL4 2ST
> Lancs
> (061) 633 6611

Appendix B

Resources for the interviewer

Books

The Body Book (1979) by Claire Rayner. London: Pan Books.
This book describes the anatomy and physiology of the human body in a way which is understandable by children 4 years and upwards. There are good line illustrations.

Anatomical Drawings by A. Nicholas Groth, illustrated by Thomas M. Stevenson, Jr. This is a collection of line drawings of naked children, adolescents and adults of different races for use in the investigation and management of child sexual abuse. It is available from:

Forensic Mental Health Associates, Inc.,
3 Ireland Road,
Newtown Center, MA 02159,
USA
(617) 332 0228

Anatomically correct dolls

These are available from:

Show and Tell Dolls,
23 Marley Comb Road,
Camelsdale,
Haslemere,
Surrey GU27 3SN
(0428) 53987

James Galt and Co. Ltd,
Brookfield Road,
Cheadle,
Cheshire SK8 2TN
(061) 428 8511

National resource organisations

The following organisations provide information on audio-visual aids and other training materials that are available for professionals. Some of them also have bibliographies and lists available on request.

National Society for the Prevention of Cruelty to Children (NSPCC)

The NSPCC has a network of child-protection teams offering services to abused children and their families in England, Wales, and Northern Ireland. At both national and local levels, the society offers a consultancy service to professionals, and provides multidisciplinary training. The Headley Library, at Saffron Hill, is a major resource centre bringing together a wide range of materials on child abuse. It can be used for reference in person, or for loans by prior arrangement. The Society's publication list is available on request. Send a large stamped addressed envelope to:

> 67 Saffron Hill,
> London EC1N 8RS
> (071) 242 1626

The National Children's Bureau (NCB)

The NCB produce a training materials resource list which includes audio-visual materials. Send a large stamped addressed envelope to:

> The National Children's Bureau,
> Child Abuse Training Unit,
> 8 Wakley Street,
> London EC1V 7QE
> (071) 278 9441

Standing Committee on Sexually Abused Children (SCOSAC)

SCOSAC produce an information pack (price on application). Please request the one for professionals. SCOSAC also produce a list of video-tapes available in the UK, as well as other information broadsheets. They have a library of approximately 100 books and 200 articles that can be referenced in person by prior arrangement. They are housed at:

> SCOSAC,
> 73 St Charles Square,
> London W10 6EJ
> (081) 960 6376

British Association for the Study and
Prevention of Child Abuse and Neglect (BASPCAN)

BASPCAN is a multidisciplinary professional organisation, which organises regional and national study days and conferences. It also publishes *Child Abuse Review*. For information contact:

> BASPCAN
> 10 Priory St,
> York YO1 1EZ
> (0904) 621133

International organisations

International Society for Prevention
of Child Abuse and Neglect (ISPCAN)

Membership includes subscription to *Child Abuse and Neglect*, a newsletter (*The Link*), and reduced registration at the biannual International Congress and European conferences. Write to:

> The Secretary,
> IPSCAN,
> 332 S. Michigan, Suite 1600,
> Chicago, IL 60604,
> USA

References

ADCOCK, M., WHITE, R. & HOLLOWS, A. (1991) *Significant Harm*. London: Significant Publications, 42 High Street, Croydon CRO 1YB.

ALLPORT, G. W. & POSTMAN, L. (1947) *The Psychology of Rumor*. New York: Henry Holt.

AMERICAN ACADEMY OF PEDIATRICS (1991) Guidelines for the evaluation of sexual abuse of children. *Pediatrics*, **87**, 254–260.

AMERICAN PSYCHIATRIC ASSOCIATION (1980) *Diagnostic and Statistical Manual of Mental Disorders* (3rd edn) (DSM–III). Washington, DC: American Psychiatric Association.

BAYS, J. (1990) Are the genitalia of anatomical dolls distorted? *Child Abuse and Neglect*, **14**, 171–176.

BECKER, J. V. & ABEL, G. G. (1984) *Methodological and Ethical Issues in Evaluating and Treating Adolescent Sexual Offenders*. Bethesda, MA: NIMH.

BENEDEK, E. P., & SCHETKY, D. H. (1985) Allegations of sexual abuse in child custody and visitation disputes. In *Emerging Issues in Child Psychiatry and the Law* (eds D. H. Schetky & E. P. Benedek). New York: Brunner/Mazel.

BERLINER, L. & BARBIERI, M. K. (1984) The testimony of the child victim of sexual assault. *Journal of Social Issues*, **40**, 125–137.

—— & CONTE, J. (1990) The process of victimisation, the victim's perspective. *Child Abuse and Neglect*, **14**, 29–40.

BOAT, B. W. & EVERSON, M. D. (1988) The use of anatomical dolls among professionals in sexual abuse evaluations. *Child Abuse and Neglect*, **12**, 171–179.

BRITTON, H. L. & O'KEEFE, M. A. (1991) Use of non-anatomical dolls in the sexual abuse interview. *Child Abuse and Neglect*, **15**, 567–573.

BROSS, D. C., KRUGMAN, R. D., LENHERR, M., *et al* (eds) (1988) *The New Child Protection Team Handbook*. New York: Garland Press.

BROWN, A. L., BRANSFORD, J. D., FERRARA, R. A., *et al* (1983) Learning, remembering and understanding. In *Handbook of Child Psychology* (eds J. H. Flavell & E. M. Maskman), pp. 77–166. New York: Wiley.

BROWNE, A. & FINKELHOR, D. (1986) Initial and long-term effects: a review of the research. In *A Sourcebook on Child Sexual Abuse* (ed. D. Finkelhor). Beverley Hills: Sage.

BURGESS, A. & HOLMSTROM, L. L. (1974) Rape trauma syndrome. *American Journal of Psychiatry*, **131**, 981–986.

—— & —— (1975) Sexual trauma of children and adolescents: sex, pressure and secrecy. *Nursing Clinics of North America*, **101**, 551–563.

—— HARTMAN, C. R., McCAUSLAND, M. P., *et al* (1984) Response patterns in children and adolescents exploited through sex rings and pornography. *American Journal of Psychiatry*, **141**, 656–662.

BUTLER-SLOSS, E. (1988) *Report of the Inquiry into Child Abuse in Cleveland in 1987*. London: HMSO.

CECI, S. J., ROSS, D. & TOGLIA, M. (1987a) Age differences in suggestibility: narrowing the uncertainties. In *Children's Eye-Witness Memory* (eds S. Ceci, M. P. Toglia & D. Ross). New York: Springer–Verlag.

——, TOGLIA, M. P. & ROSS, D. (1987b) *Children's Eye-Witness Memory*. New York: Springer–Verlag.

COLE, C. B. & LOFTUS, E. F. (1987) The memory of children. In *Children's Eye-Witness Memory* (eds S. Ceci, M. P. Toglia & D. Ross). New York: Springer–Verlag.

CONTE, J. R., BERLINER, L. & SCHUERMANN, J. R. (1987) *The Impact of Sexual Abuse on Children: Final Technical Report*. Bethesda, MA: NIMH.

—— & —— (1988) The impact of sexual abuse on children: clinical findings. In *Handbook on Sexual Abuse of Children: Assessment and Treatment Issues* (ed. L. Walker). New York: Springer.

——, WOLFE, S. & SMITH, T. (1989) What sexual offenders tell us about prevention strategies. *Child Abuse and Neglect*, **13**, 293–301.

COX, A. & RUTTER, M. (1985) Diagnostic appraisal and interviewing. In *Child and Adolescent Psychiatry, Modern Approaches* (eds M. Rutter & L. Hersov). London: Blackwell.

DALE, P. S., LOFTUS, E. F. & RATHBUN, L. (1978) The influence of the form of the question on the eyewitness testimony of preschool children. *Journal of Psycholinguistic Research*, **7**, 269–277.

DAVIES, G., STEPHENSON-ROBB, Y. & FLINN, R. (1986) The reliability of children's testimony. *International Legal Practitioner*, 95–103.

DENT, H. R. (1982) The effects of interviewing strategies on the results of interviews with child witnesses. In *Reconstructing the Past: The Role of Psychologists in Criminal Trials* (ed. A. Trankell). Stockholm: Norstedt.

—— & STEPHENSON, G. M. (1979) An experimental study of the effectiveness of different techniques of questioning child witnesses. *British Journal of Social and Clinical Psychology*, **18**, 41–51.

DEPARTMENT OF HEALTH (1988) *Diagnosis of Child Sexual Abuse: Guidance for Doctors. Report Prepared by the Standing Medical Advisory Committee*. London: HMSO.

—— (1988) *Protecting Children: A Guide for Social Workers Undertaking a Comprehensive Assessment*. London: HMSO.

—— (1991) *Working Together under The Children Act 1989; a Guide to Arrangements for Inter-agency Cooperation for the Protection of Children from Abuse*. London: HMSO.

DONALDSON, M. (1978) *Children's Minds*. Glasgow: Fontana.

EVERSON, M. D. & BOAT, B. W. (1990) Sexualised doll play among young children: implications for the use of anatomical dolls in sexual abuse evaluations. *Journal of the American Academy of Child and Adolescent Psychiatry*, **29**, 736–742.

EVERSTINE, D. S. & EVERSTINE, L. (1983) The adult woman victim of rape. In *People in Crisis: Strategic Therapeutic Interventions* (eds D. S. Everstine & L. Everstine). New York: Brunner Mazel.

FALLER, K. C. (1984) Is the child victim of sexual abuse telling the truth? *Child Abuse and Neglect*, **8**, 473–481.

—— (1990) *Understanding Child Sexual Maltreatment*. London: Sage.

FINKELHOR, D. (1979) *Sexually Victimized Children*. New York: Free Press.

—— (1984) Four preconditions of sexual abuse: a model. In *Child Sexual Abuse; New Theory and Research* (ed. D. Finkelhor). New York: Free Press.

FLIN, R. (1990) Child witnesses in criminal courts. *Children and Society*, **4**, 264–283.

FRASER, B. G. (1981) Sexual child abuse: legislation and law in the United States. In *Sexually Abused Children and Their Families* (eds P. B. Mrazek & C. H. Kempe). Oxford: Pergamon.

FRIEDRICH, W. N. (1990) *Psychotherapy of Sexually Abused Children and their Families*. London: W. W. Norton.

——, BEILKE, R. L. & URQUIZA, A. J. (1987) Children from sexually abusive families: a behavioural comparison. *Journal of Interpersonal Violence*, **2**, 391–402.

GARVEY, C. (1977) *Play* (in the "Developing Child Series"). Cambridge, MA: Harvard University Press.

GELINAS, D. J. (1983) The persisting negative effects of incest. *Psychiatry*, **46**, 312–332.

GELMAN, R. (1978) Cognitive development. *Annual Review of Psychology*, **29**, 297–332.

GIARRETTO, H. (1976) Humanistic treatment of father–daughter incest. In *Child Abuse and Neglect: The Family and the Community* (eds R. E. Helfer & C. H. Kempe), pp. 143–168. Cambridge, MA: Ballinger.

GLASER, D. & COLLINS, C. (1989) The response of young, non-sexually abused children to anatomically correct dolls. *Journal of Child Psychology and Psychiatry*, **30**, 547–560.

GOMES-SCHWARTZ, B., HOROWITZ, J. M. & SAUZIER, M. (1985) Severity of emotional distress among sexually abused pre-school, school age and adolescent children. *Hospital and Community Psychiatry*, **36**, 503–508.

GOODMAN, G. S. (1984) The child witness: conclusions and future directions for research and legal practice. *Journal of Social Issues*, **40**, 157–175.

—— & HELGESON, V. S. (1985) Child sexual assault: children's memory and the law. *University of Miami Law Review*, **40**, 181–208.

—— & JONES, D. P. H. (1988) The emotional effects of criminal court testimony on child sexual assault victims: a preliminary report. In *The Child Witness: Do the Courts Abuse Children* (ed. G. Davies & J. Drinkwater). Leicester: British Psychological Society. *Issues in Criminological and Legal Psychology*, no. 13.

—— & AMAN, C. (1990) Children's use of anatomically detailed dolls to recount an event. *Child Development*, **61**, 1859–1871.

—— & CLARKE-STEWART, A. (1990) Suggestibility in children's testimony: implications for sexual abuse investigations. In *The Suggestibility of Children's Recollections* (ed. J. Doris). Washington, DC: American Psychological Association.

GOODWIN, J. (1982) The use of drawings in incest cases. In *Sexual Abuse: Incest Victims and Their Families* (ed. J. Goodwin), pp. 47–56. London: John Wright.

——, SAHD, D. & RADA, R. T. (1982) False accusations and false denials of incest: clinical myths and clinical realities. In *Sexual Abuse: Incest Victims and Their Families* (ed. J. Goodwin), pp. 17–26. London: John Wright.

GREEN, A. H. (1986) True and false allegations of sexual abuse in child custody disputes. *Journal of the American Academy of Child Psychiatry*, **25**, 449–456.

GREENSPAN, S. (1981) *The Clinical Interview of the Child.* London: McGraw-Hill.

GUDJONSSON, G. H. & GUNN, J. (1982) The competence and reliability of a witness in a criminal court: a case report. *British Journal of Psychiatry*, **141**, 624–627.

HALEY, J. (1973) *Uncommon Therapy: The Psychiatric Techniques of Milton Erickson.* New York: Norton.

HEIMAN, M. L. (1992) Putting the puzzle together: validating allegations of child sexual abuse. *Journal of Child Psychology and Psychiatry*, **33**, 311–329.

HELFER, R. & KEMPE, R. (eds) (1987) *The Battered Child* (4th edn). Chicago: University of Chicago Press.

HILL, P. (1985) The diagnostic interview with the individual child. In *Child and Adolescent Psychiatry, Modern Approaches* (eds M. Rutter & L. Hersov). London: Blackwell.

HOME OFFICE (1992) *Memorandum of Good Practice: Video Recorded Interviews with Child Witnesses for Criminal Proceedings.* London: HMSO.

JAMES, J. & MEYERDING, J. (1977) Early sexual experience and prostitution. *American Journal of Psychiatry*, **134**, 1381–1385.

JAMPOLE, L. & WEBER, M. K. (1987) An assessment of the behaviour of sexually abused and non-sexually abused children with anatomically correct dolls. *Child Abuse and Neglect*, **11**, 187–192.

JOHNSON, M. K. & FOLEY, M. A. (1984) Differentiating fact from fantasy: the reliability of children's memory. *Journal of Social Issues*, **40**, 33–50.

JONES, D. P. H. (1986) Individual psychotherapy for the sexually abused child. *Child Abuse and Neglect*, **10**, 377–385.

—— (1989) Some reflections on the Cleveland affair. *Association of Child Psychology and Psychiatry Newsletter*, **11**, 13–18.

—— (1991) Working with the children act: tasks and responsibilities of the child and adolescent psychiatrist. In *Proceedings of the Children Act Course* (ed. C. Lindsey), Occasional Paper no. 12. London: Royal College of Psychiatrists.

—— & KRUGMAN, R. (1986) Can a three-year-old child bear witness to her sexual assault and attempted murder? *Child Abuse and Neglect*, **10**, 253–258.

—— & McGRAW, J. M. (1987) Reliable and fictitious accounts of sexual abuse to children. *Journal of Interpersonal Violence*, **2**, 27–45.

—— & SEIG, A. (1988) Child sexual abuse allegations in custody or visitation disputes. In *Sexual Abuse Allegations in Custody and Visitation Disputes* (ed. B. Nicholson). Washington, DC: American Bar Association.

——, KEMPE, R. S. & STEELE, B. F. (1988) The psychiatric evaluation and treatment plan. In *The New Child Protection Team Handbook* (eds D. Bross *et al*). New York: Garland.

—— & THOMPSON, P. J. (1991) Children's sexual experience – normal and abnormal. In *Paediatric Specialty Practice 1991* (eds J. Eyre & R. Boyd). London: Royal College of Physicians.

KENDALL-TACKETT, K. A. (1992) Beyond anatomical dolls: professionals' use of other play therapy techniques. *Child Abuse and Neglect*, **16**, 139–142.

KING, M. A. & YUILLE, J. C. (1987) Suggestibility and the child witness. In *Children's Eye-Witness Memory* (eds S. Ceci, M. P. Toglia & D. Ross). New York: Springer–Verlag.

KIRBY, R. & RADFORD, J. (1976) *Individual Differences*. London: Methuen.

KOLVIN, I., STEINER, H., BAMFORD, F., *et al* (1988) Child sexual abuse – some principles of good practice. *British Journal of Hospital Medicine*, **39**, 54–62.

LANKTREE, C., BRIERE, J. & ZAIDI, L. (1991) Incidence and impact of sexual abuse in a child outpatient sample: the role of direct inquiry. *Child Abuse and Neglect*, **15**, 447–454.

LEVENTHAL, J. M., BENTOVIM, A., ELTON, A., *et al* (1987) What to ask when sexual abuse is suspected. *Archives of Disease in Childhood*, **62**, 1188–1195.

LINDBERG, M. (1980) Is knowledge base development a necessary and sufficient condition for memory development? *Journal of Experimental Child Psychology*, **30**, 401–410.

LISTER, E. D. (1982) Forced silence: a neglected dimension of trauma. *American Journal of Psychiatry*, **139**, 867–872.

LOFTUS, E. F. & DAVIES, G. M. (1984) Distortions in the memory of children. *Journal of Social Issues*, **40**, 51–67.

LUKIANOWICZ, N. (1972) Incest I – paternal incest; II – other types of incest. *British Journal of Psychiatry*, **120**, 301–313.

MACFARLANE, K. (1985) Diagnostic evaluations and the use of videotapes in child sexual abuse cases. *University Of Miami Law Review*. **40**, 135–165.

MARIN, B. V., HOLMES, D. L., GUTH, M., *et al* (1979) The potential of children as eye witnesses. *Law and Human Behavior*, **3**, 295–306.

McGURK, H. (1975) *Growing and Changing*. London: Methuen.

MEHTA, M. N., LOKESHWAR, M. R., BHATT, S. C., *et al* (1979) Rape in children. *Child Abuse and Neglect*, **3**, 671–677.

McLEER, S., DEBLINGER, E., ATKINS, M., *et al* (1988) Post traumatic stress disorder in sexually abused children. *Journal of the American Academy of Child and Adolescent Psychiatry*, **27**, 650–654.

MEISELMAN, K. C. (1978) *Incest: A Psychological Study of Causes and Effects with Treatment Recommendations*. San Francisco: Jossey Bass.

MELTON, G., BULKLEY, J. & WULKAR, D. (1981) Competency of children as witnesses. In *Child Sexual Abuse and the Law* (ed. J. Bulkley), pp. 125–145. Washington, DC: American Bar Association.

MOORE, J. & KENDALL, D. G. (1971) Children's concepts of reproduction. *Journal of Sex Research*, **7**, 42–61.

MOSTON, S. (1990) How children interpret and respond to questions: situational sources of suggestibility in eyewitness interviews. *Social Behaviour*, **5**, 155–167.

MRAZEK, P. B. (1981) Definition and recognition of sexual child abuse. In *Sexually Abused Children and Their Families* (ed. P. B. Mrazek & C. H. Kempe). Oxford: Pergamon Press.

—— & KEMPE, C. H. (eds) (1981) *Sexually Abused Children and Their Families*. Oxford: Pergamon Press.

MUSSEN, P. H., CONGER, J. J., KAGAN, J., *et al* (1984) *Child Development and Personality*. New York: Harper and Row.

NAITORE, C. E. (1982) Art therapy with sexually abused children. In *Handbook of Clinical Intervention in Child Sexual Abuse* (ed. S. M. Sgroi), pp. 269–308. Lexington, MA: D. C. Heath.

NEINSTEIN, L. S., GOLDENRING, J. & CARPENTER, S. (1984) Nonsexual transmission of sexually transmitted diseases: an infrequent occurrence. *Paediatrics*, **74**, 67–76.

OXFORDSHIRE AREA CHILD PROTECTION COMMITTEE (1992) *Child Protection Procedures*. Oxford: Oxfordshire Social Services Department.

OUNSTED, C. & LYNCH, M. (1976) Family pathology as seen in England. In *Child Abuse and Neglect: The Family and the Community* (eds R. E. Helfer & C. H. Kempe), pp. 75–86. Cambridge, MA: Ballinger.

PERLMUTTER, M. (ed.) (1980) *Children's Memory. New Directions in Child Development*, no. 10. San Francisco, CA: Jossey–Bass.

PETERSON, C. & SELIGMAN, M. E. P. (1983) Learned helplessness and victimization. *Journal of Social Issues*, **39**, 103–116.

PIPE, M-E. & GOODMAN, G. S. (1991) Elements of secrecy: implications for children's testimony. *Behavioral Sciences and the Law*, **9**, 33–41.

PIZZEY, E. (1974) *Scream Quietly or the Neighbours Will Hear*. London: Penguin.

PORTER, F. S., BLICK, L. C. & SGROI, S. M. (1982) Treatment of the sexually abused child. In *Handbook of Clinical Intervention in Child Sexual Abuse* (ed. S. M. Sgroi), pp. 109–145. Lexington, MA: D. C. Heath.

PRICE, D. W. W. (1984) "The development of children's comprehension of recurring episodes." Doctoral dissertation, University of Denver, CO.

PYNOOS, R. S. & ETH, S. (1984) The child as witness to homicide. *Journal of Social Issues*, **40**, 87–108.

ROSENBLATT, D. B. (1980) Play. In *Scientific Foundations of Developmental Psychiatry* (ed. M. Rutter). London: Heinemann.

ROSENFELD, A., BAILEY, R., SIEGEL, B., *et al* (1986) Determining incestuous contact between parent and child: frequency of children touching parents' genitals in a non-clinical population. *Journal of the American Academy of Child Psychiatry*, **25**, 481–484.

ROYAL COLLEGE OF PHYSICIANS (1991) *Physical Signs of Sexual Abuse in Children*. London: Royal College of Physicians.

ROYAL COLLEGE OF PSYCHIATRISTS (1988) Child psychiatric perspectives on the assessment and management of sexually abused children. *Bulletin of the Royal College of Psychiatrists*, **12**, 534–540.

RUBIN, K. H., FEIN, G. G. & VANDENBURY, B. (1983) Play. In *Handbook of Child Psychology* (ed. P. H. Mussen), vol. iv. Chichester: John Wiley.

RUSSELL, D. E. H. (1986) *The Secret Trauma: Incest in the Lives of Girls and Women*. New York: Basic Books.

RUTTER, M. (1980) Psychosexual development. In *Scientific Foundations of Developmental Psychiatry* (ed. M. Rutter). London: Heinemann.

—— (1985) Resilience in the face of adversity; protective factors and psychiatric disorder. *British Journal of Psychiatry*, **147**, 598–611.

SCHECTER, M. D. & ROBERGE, L. (1986) Sexual exploitation. In *Child Abuse and Neglect: The Family and the Community* (eds R. E. Helfer & C. H. Kempe). Cambridge, MA: Ballinger.

SGROI, M. (1982) *Handbook of Clinical Intervention in Child Sexual Abuse*. Lexington, MA: D. C. Heath.

——, PORTER, F. S. & BLICK, L. C. (1982) Validation of child sexual abuse. In *Handbook of Clinical Intervention in Child Sexual Abuse* (ed. S. M. Sgroi), pp. 39–79. Lexington, MA: D. C. Heath.

SHENGOLD, L. (1967) The effects of overstimulation: rat people. *International Journal of Psychoanalysis*, **48**, 403–415.

SIMPSON, C. A., & PORTER, G. L. (1981) Self-mutilation in children and adolescents. *Bulletin of the Meninger Clinic*, **45**, 428–438.

SIVAN, A. B., SCHOR, D. P., KOEPPL, G. K., *et al* (1988) Interaction of normal children with anatomical dolls. *Child Abuse and Neglect*, **12**, 295–304.

SORENSEN, T. & SNOW, B. (1991) How children tell: the process of disclosure in child sexual abuse. *Child Welfare*, **70**, 3–15.

STEMBER, C. J. (1980) Art therapy: a new use in the diagnosis and treatment of sexually abused children. In *Sexual Abuse of Children: Selected Readings*. Washington, DC: US Department of Health and Human Services.

SUMMIT, R. (1983) The child sexual abuse accommodation syndrome. *Child Abuse and Neglect*, **7**, 177–193.

TAYLOR, D. C. (1982) The components of sickness: diseases, illnesses and predicaments. In *One Child* (eds J. Apley & C. Ounsted), pp. 1–13. London: Heinemann.

TERR, L. (1979) Children of Chowchilla: Study of psychic trauma. *Psychoanalytic Study of the Child*, **34**, 547–623.

TIZARD, B. & HARVEY, D. (1977) *The Biology of Play*. London: Heinemann, SIMP.

TODD, C. M. & PERLMUTTER, M. (1980) Reality recalled by preschool children. In *Children's Memory: New Directions in Child Development*, no. 10, pp. 69–85. San Francisco, CA: Jossey–Bass.

TULLY, B. & CAHILL, D. (1984) *Police Interviewing of the Mentally Handicapped*. London: Police Foundation.

TYLER, A. H. & BRASSARD, M. R. (1984) Abuse in the investigation and treatment of intrafamilial child sexual abuse. *Child Abuse and Neglect*, **81**, 47–53.

UNDEUTSCH, V. (1982) Statement reality analysis. In *Reconstructing the Past: The Role of Psychologists in Criminal Trials* (ed. A. Trankell), pp. 27–56. Stockholm: P. A. Norsted.

VIZARD, E., BENTOVIM, A. & TRANTER, M. (1987) Interviewing sexually abused children. *Adoption and Fostering*, **11**, 20–25.

WATERMAN, J. (1986) Developmental considerations. In *Sexual Abuse of Young Children* (eds K. MacFarlane *et al*). London: Guilford Press.

WHITE, S., STROM, G. A., SANTILLI, G., *et al* (1986) Interviewing young sexual abuse victims with anatomically correct dolls. *Child Abuse and Neglect*, **10**, 519–529.

WINNICOTT, D. W. (1971) *Therapeutic Consultations in Child Psychiatry*. London: Hogarth Press.

ZARAGOZA, M. S. (1987) Memory suggestibility and eye-witness testimony in children and adults. In *Children's Eye-Witness Memory* (eds S. Ceci, M. P. Toglia & D. Ross). New York: Springer–Verlag.

Gaskell Books

Evaluation of Comprehensive Care of the Mentally Ill
Edited by Hugh Freeman & John Henderson
£7.50, 224pp., 1991

Mental Health Services in the Global Village
Edited by Louis Appleby & Ricardo Araya
£10.00, 224pp., 1991

150 Years of British Psychiatry, 1841–1991
Edited by German E. Berrios & Hugh Freeman
£15.00, 464pp., 1991

Child Psychiatry and the Law (second edition)
Edited by Dora Black, Stephen Wolkind &
Jean Harris Hendriks
£10.00, 200pp., 1991

The Use of Drugs in Psychiatry (third edition)
By John Crammer & Bernard Heine
£6.50, 256pp., 1991

Concepts of Mental Disorder. A Continuing Debate
Edited by Alan Kerr & Hamish McClelland
£7.50, 160pp., 1991

The Closure of Mental Hospitals
Edited by Peter Hall & Ian F. Brockington
£7.50, 160pp., 1991

Dysthymic Disorder
Edited by S. W. Burton & H. S. Akiskal
£7.50, 144pp., 1990

A catalogue of all Gaskell publications and details of any of the above titles are available from Gaskell, Royal College of Psychiatrists, 17 Belgrave Square, London SW1X 8PG.